UNDERSTANDING BALLET

UNDERSTANDING BALLET

by Mary Clarke and Clement Crisp

With a foreword by Natalia Makarova

Harmony Books

New York

on title page The corps de ballet of The Royal Ballet in *La Bayadère*. It was because of performances as immaculate as this that the Royal corps de ballet was awarded the London *Evening Standard*'s annual ballet award for 1974. The authors of this book were members of the panel and, although 1974 had been an exciting year for ballet in Britain, it was the unanimous decision of the panel that the achievement of the Royal corps as a magnificent ensemble outshone everything else.

Sources of illustration

Page 56 photograph by Baron Studios; page 13, 40, 54, 67, 69, 81, 84 *bottom*, 99 by Anthony Crickmay; titlepage, page 15, 18, by Zoë Dominic; page 35, 42 *bottom* by Fred Fehl; page 84 *top* by Daniel Keryzaouen; page 88 by Peggy Leder; page 83 by Serge Lido; page 29 from Ray Mander and Joe Mitchenson Collection; page 79 by Marchioni; page 30 by H. J. Mydtskov; page 44 from the New Arts Management; page 42 *top* by Stuart Robinson; page 39, 59, 65 by Houston Rogers; page 63 by Roy Round; page 32 by Ezra Stoller; page 37 by Martha Swope; page 12 from Paul Taylor Dance Foundation; page 21, 24 by Reg Wilson; page 58 by Roger Wood.

All Rights Reserved. No part of this book may be reproduced or utilized by any means, electronic or mechanical, including photocopying, recording or by any information storage and retrieval system without permission in writing from the Publisher. Inquiries should be addressed to:

Harmony Books
a division of Crown Publishers, Inc.
419 Park Avenue South
New York, New York
10016

Published simultaneously in Canada by
General Publishing Company Limited.
First published in the UK by Studio Vista, a division of
Cassell and Collier Macmillan Publishers Ltd.

Printed in Great Britain
Second printing

Library of Congress Cataloging in Publication Data
Clarke, Mary
    Understanding ballet.
1. Ballet-History. I. Crisp, Clement, joint author.
II. Title
GV1787.C7   792.8'09   75-10952
ISBN 0-517-52650-6
ISBN 0-517-52649-2

CONTENTS

ON BEING
A DANCER

by Natalia Makarova

I think that dancing is the most natural way to express feeling. With very primitive people and tribes, they move to express themselves. But that is not ballet, yet; that is dancing. Ballet is 'framed'; it is the professional way of using this movement, and you make art from this natural thing. Just as you make a sculpture from a piece of beautiful stone, so you make ballet from the natural quality of movement.

People don't need to 'understand' ballet. They must simply look, and they will either feel something, or they will not. They do not need to know how the steps are named: if they find expressiveness coming from the stage and can catch it and become involved with it, that is the very best thing that ballet can do.

A sculptor or a writer doesn't need to tell how he works – it is the result of his work that matters. But of course people want to know more: they like to take machines apart. When I was a little girl I used always to take my dolls apart to try and see what was inside them. And so we want to analyse dancing; I don't think people will *feel* anything more if they understand; but they will *appreciate* more. Perhaps they will understand that ballet is not easy. Dancing is easy in the ballroom because you are continuing your natural way of movement. But when dancing becomes art – in the theatre – it is not easy at all! It is the hardest thing in the world. I don't know of anything that can be compared with it for difficulty. It is complex, and elusive, even technique. One day, everything you have studied and learned about technique can work and be good. The next – you feel ill, or emotionally wrong, and the dancing becomes awful. You cannot correct it, even. No one can. You try, and you know that because you are a professional and have studied, it won't fall below a certain standard, but it is still not *good*. You can't help yourself, and your body won't listen to what you tell it. In the other arts you can rest and clear your mind and think about *how* to work. But if you rest in ballet, you lose everything; and, also, if you work too hard you lose something too. And your body hurts. You can plan a vacation and go away, and all the time you are on holiday you are thinking: 'It will be so *terrible* when I get back to work', and so you worry all the time and your vacation does you no good at all.

Dancing becomes a kind of religion for us, and also a form of masochism. Without that quality I don't know how you can improve yourself. You must enjoy the suffering of being a dancer. And there are bad times – I know that even if I put all my concentration and effort into something I want to achieve the result is never immediate. You work on something so that some day there will be a result – but it is a long-term result. When I was a young dancer I was impatient and looked for immediate results; and I never got them. Then suddenly, after a year, there came the result of what I had done a year before. Dancing is an exciting life, but terrifyingly difficult. But at least it doesn't allow us to be 'empty' inside. Sometimes people seem to me to be afraid of themselves because they feel empty inside. But dancers are so concentrated in their efforts of mind and body, and so busy exploring their abilities, that they haven't time to worry about searching for something to satisfy themselves. They are searching to give the best of themselves to the public, and to dancing.

INTRODUCTION

One world-famous choreographer calls his dances food for the eyes; another asks his audiences just to come and look. And the main reason for going to the ballet is simply that dancing is such tremendous fun to watch. You see beautiful bodies doing beautiful things. You can hear all kinds of music from symphonies to pop. You can see designs created by some of the greatest painters of this century. Above all you can be thrilled or moved by the fact that the human body can tell a story or create a mood, can make you laugh or cry without the help of words. Indeed you realize that only in ballet are there certain marvellous pleasures to be found, such as the sight of a superbly trained body whirling and leaping in harmony with music, and the actual joy that can be communicated by the power of the human body as it moves across a stage.

It is extraordinary that some people seem frightened of the word ballet. We have learned that it is safest, when asked 'What do you do?' not to mention the word 'ballet' but to say 'We write about dancing'. We are very surprised that so many people are still puzzled by ballet: they are not prepared to enjoy it as they will enjoy gymnastics, skating or athletics, or even ballroom dancing. These are all physical displays which fascinate and excite the onlooker because highly trained bodies are doing beautiful things with immense skill. You look, you marvel and you do not ask any questions about the whys and wherefores. If only people looked at theatrical dancing in this way we should not be writing this book, but a lot more people would enjoy ballet for the right reasons.

It is the decision to go to the ballet – to make a start – that counts. Once you have gone into the theatre, be it your local one or a very grand opera house, and your interest and enthusiasm have been aroused, you can begin a career as a balletomane. From then on it is a question of money, of course, quite as much as it is of inclination, but if you take advantage of the many schemes that now exist to assist people, especially students and young people, to go to the theatre, you should be able to see quite a few performances without impoverishing yourself. The subsidised dance companies have a very good record of maintaining lower seat prices in some parts of the theatre, and indeed a seat at The Royal Opera House can be as cheap as a seat in a London cinema.

Ballet going is renowned to be addictive, and this is how the addiction starts – you go once; you go again. You want to know more so you go to the library and start to browse. You then see another ballet company and realize something of the range of dance. You go again – and you become an addict. Thus you have joined the band of enthusiasts that stretches back to the very beginnings of ballet and includes kings and poets, people who have had a dancer's shoes cooked and then eaten them, students who have pulled ballerinas in their carriages through the streets; and a great many people like us who have found that ballet can be the most rewarding and wonderful of obsessions. You have also joined an international club. In Leningrad, New York, Tokyo and Brussels the real balletgoers speak the same language. There is a camaraderie that exists between ballet fans that can make them firm friends after just one meeting. There is always something to discuss. By introducing you to the basic concepts involved in ballet, we hope that you will be able to join in these discussions.

We hope that this book will answer the questions asked by newcomers to ballet. It gives a short history of ballet and ballet companies, and describes the kind of training that the dancers have and the life they lead, and outlines the preparation that leads up to a performance and the work of creating a new ballet. However, the book is intended as an introduction, and we hope you will go on to read and find out more about your particular interests as they develop.

THE
DANCERS

Just as every recipe in a cookery book begins with the ingredients, a guide to the ballets should start with the essential raw material of the performance. Although ballets are sometimes danced without music or without decor – and sometimes without costumes – they simply cannot be danced without dancers. This is a rather bald statement but one which has to be stressed from the very beginning. Dancers are athletes; they are athletes whose training is harder, more demanding and much, much longer than any gymnast's or sprinter's. Like footballers, they must train throughout their career, but unlike most other athletes, dancers have no closed season. The daily class which usually lasts for an hour and a half continues right through their active careers. From their entry into the ballet school until the day they take off their dancing shoes for the last time, dancers know that every weekday will begin with the same sweating ritual of bending and stretching and teaching their bodies. The only time off is annual or public holidays and Sundays or another day of rest in the week. A dancer once said, 'If I miss class for one day I know it; if I miss class for two days the audience will know it'. And this applies to the greatest as well as the humblest members of a company.

The training
On any level ballet training is good for the body. Boys or girls attending just a weekly ballet class will stand a little straighter, keep a little slimmer, look a little more alert. The physical discipline that is the essence of ballet training can bring mental discipline too. But there are no short cuts; either a limb is properly stretched, a foot properly pointed, or it is not. And for the child who seems gifted enough (physically and mentally) to take up ballet as a career there are no

An athlete and an athlete/dancer. We accept the skill and agility of a goalkeeper saving the ball. What people often do not realise is the even greater skill and greater athletic prowess of a dancer like the American, Paul Taylor, seen here with members of his company.

Even for a dancer as great as Dame Margot Fonteyn, daily class never ceases. Here she is practising in one of the studios of The Royal Ballet School.

halfway houses. From the very beginning ballet training needs determination and dedication.

Ballet training can start with baby classes but these are gentle and do little more than encourage good posture and perhaps foster an understanding of music. By the time a child reaches the age of about eleven any chance of becoming a dancer will be apparent. The schools attached to the great national companies audition youngsters at this time. These auditions are not concerned with prior training, only with the intelligence and the actual physique of the candidate. Rigorous medical examination will show if the body is suitable for classical training because the least and smallest physical defect (a bone slightly out of alignment, a family tradition of exceptional tallness) can mean that ultimately the child will not be able to make a career in classical ballet. For example, a boy with a brilliant record in children's stage dancing competitions

was turned down by The Royal Ballet School because weakness at the back of one knee could have resulted in serious injury when he came to the rigours of partnering. There was no reason, though, why he should not have made a career in other forms of theatre dance such as jazz or musical comedy.

Most schools attached to the national ballet companies throughout the world give their young pupils a combination of academic and ballet training during their first five years. The academic schooling is important since there is inevitably a weeding out of apprentice dancers whose promise is not fulfilled and it is essential even for the successful students to have a sound education.

Ballet training itself is a system of movement that has been developed over a period of three hundred years, but it is important to insist that the classical technique that students learn is an entirely logical and sensible method of movement. Its aim is to achieve maximum control and maximum mobility. 'Turn out' is the first basic principle of ballet training. The leg is taught to turn out from the hip socket to an angle of 90° to gain freedom of movement and pleasing line. By giving the legs the greatest possible flexibility it enormously increases the range of movement of a dancer's body. Good turn out is acquired easily and without strain, from the hip, never from the knee. All the other controls and disciplines aim at a similar command of the body's actions. All have been proved over the years. None can be ignored, though it would be foolhardy to suggest that they cannot be improved.

It is very important that even early training should be undertaken in a school where the teachers are properly qualified and have themselves been trained either by one of the several good teaching bodies – like the Royal Academy of Dancing or the Imperial Society – or by previous experience as a dancer from a major ballet company. Care in early training is absolutely vital. A bad muscular habit or bad positioning can result in physical injury and perhaps deprive a student of a later career as a professional dancer. Faults acquired at a very early age can only sometimes be eradicated; sound basic training, on the other hand, is the foundation for the dancer's entire career.

The degree of movement of which the human body is capable depends on the flexibility and strength of the muscles and on the length of the ligaments (bone-connecting tissues). Ligaments are not flexible, like muscles, but they can be lengthened by special training at an early age before they have had time to harden. This is one reason why the professional dancer needs to start training young. The least flexible part of the body is the skeleton, the bony frame. The structure of bones and joints governs the amount of bodily movement in any one direction. The ribs and chest can easily be bent to each side and forwards but will not bend back. The ball and socket structure of the shoulder and hip joints permit a degree of movement. Movement from the hip is easier in a forward direction; it is more difficult to swing the leg up to the side or the back than in front of the body. The ballet dancer must practise until it can be raised high in all directions without any loss of balance or control. The secret in dancing – as in, say, water skiing – is in the control of distribution of weight. Although the ballet

At England's Royal Ballet School, the boys learn not only the disciplines of classical dancing but they are also expected to be sportsmen. This is a beautiful example of a Flying Angel in a gymnastics class.

dancer trains every part of the body, special care is given to the feet and legs. The dancer's foot is a springboard and only from the strength in the feet and legs can the body be propelled into the air, or achieve and maintain all the positions and movements required of it. For girls there will be the additional demands of pointe work. Girls are trained very carefully to prepare to go on pointe and only do so when strong enough (usually at about the age of thirteen) and in well chosen pointe shoes. First they do exercises to accustom themselves to balancing effortlessly on pointe and then they begin the actual steps and turns. In all pointe work there is the basic consideration of 'placing', each dancer must find her centre of equilibrium; if she is at all off balance, injuries and falls will inevitably follow. The hours of hard work and exercise are designed to help the dancer defy the laws of gravity, to leap high in the air, to perform intricate beating movements of the feet (batterie), to alight softly and surely and with sufficient control to go straight into a fast series of multiple turns (pirouettes), and to acquire harmonious movements of the arms and changes of direction of the head and shoulders (épaulement).

At the age of sixteen or thereabouts the full-time professional dance training commences and during the next couple of years takes up the greater part of the student's day. The culmination comes in the final year when the student will

These third year students in the Bolshoy School in Moscow are already sufficiently strong to be making their first exercises on pointe.

either be accepted into the company or will have to seek work elsewhere, be it in another ballet company or in some other form of show business.

The dancer's instrument, we must stress and stress again, is the human body, and the way in which it can be used depends almost entirely on how it has – or has not – been trained. It is possible to devise very beautiful and striking ensemble works with dancers who have had virtually no training but who can look and move well. A clever choreographer can manipulate them into sculptural poses or groups. Many Nativity plays, for example, have used untrained dancers to very good effect. But the trained body is nearly always more eloquent and permits much greater variety of steps, jumps, turns, lifts and almost acrobatic skills. The classical ballet dancer has a remarkable range of movement that cannot be attempted by ordinary mortals.

The dancer's life

One of the reasons why ballet seems a foreign country to so many people is that the dancer's life is a very 'enclosed' one. The training is still conducted in a foreign language since all dance steps are known throughout the world by the French terminology. In addition, the exhausting routine of the dancers' day means that they have even less time than musicians or actors to look beyond their own very private world of class, rehearsal and performance. In Britain and America the dancer's day may differ a little from that of their colleagues in Europe in the hours they are free to go about their own business, to shop, read, relax or entertain – but in the main the routine is the same throughout the world. It begins with morning class, which should be attended by every member of the company. This hour and a half is the warm-up and preparation for the rehearsals that must inevitably follow. Dancers have to keep their bodies warm and so they usually start class heavily swathed in woolly cross-over bodices and knitted leg warmers which they gradually discard as the physical effort warms them. Practice dress is usually plain tights and leotards or tunics for the girls and sweat shirts for the boys. It is essential that dancers' hair is tightly bound for class so that neck muscles are visible to the teacher. The purpose of practice wear is to give the dancers freedom of movement and the teacher ability to see faults in placing.

Class begins with the first messages to the muscles and ligaments and joints that demands are going to be made upon them. With very gradual bendings and stretchings at the barre, blood and oxygen are pumped round the body. Slowly the machine is warmed up. Just as a motor car cannot start in top gear, so too a dancer's body has to be slowly prepared for the more difficult steps and exercises that come at the end of a class. Men and women do the same basic class. After the initial exercises at the barre they progress to unsupported centre work, beginning with adage which develops balance, control, line and ports de bras. Then come the steps of virtuosity, the leaps and turns that are so often the pinnacle of excitement on stage. As the exercises develop, different demands are

The start of the dancer's day. Our picture shows the artists of The Royal Ballet in class, during the company's visit to Russia in 1961. In the front are four ballerinas, Nadia Nerina, Dame Margot Fonteyn, Annette Page and Svetlana Beriosova.

made upon the dancers' bodies – the last part of the class for the women, for instance, will be pointe work.

With class over, the dancers' day has started. Since every ballet company relies upon a large and varied repertory of constantly changing ballets, it is the task of the production and teaching staff to make sure that these works are kept in the right condition for the public to see them. This means that time must be set aside every day to rehearse them, to make sure that every member of the cast knows his or her role, that new dancers are taught the choreography and that leading dancers in the ballets are given the special coaching which they must have. Time must also be found for the creation of new ballets and, since it can often happen that two minutes of the choreography we see in performance are the result of several hours of rehearsal, arrangements also have to be made for the choreographer and his chosen dancers to work undisturbed. Because nearly every ballet company lacks rehearsal space, this may mean that dancers shuttle from studio to rehearsal room or theatre in order to keep up with the tremendous demands on their time. When you add to this the additional problems of costume fitting, photographic sessions, and, for many dancers, the extra difficulties of being on tour, you may understand that a dancer's life is a constant battle against exhaustion. Contrary to popular belief, professional dancers do not have to diet to keep slim, more usually they have to eat very well indeed to sustain their energies.

By five o'clock in the afternoon thoughts must turn towards the theatre, and for the junior members of the company, the corps de ballet, this means performance. (Soloists and principals in European companies have more time off, and in certain companies where ballet shares a theatre with opera, the dancers will at least be able to call some evenings in the week their own.)

The question of rank in a ballet company is quite simple. Traditionally a company is led by a group of principal dancers, its stars. These are the ballerinas (more of this word in a moment) and the premiers danseurs who will take the leading roles. Under them are the soloists, aspirants for stardom, who perform the secondary roles in ballets – often quite important. Also in larger companies there may be other ranks such as 'second soloists'. All these rest upon the essential foundation of the corps de ballet. The rules are not hard and fast, however: soloists can dance leading roles, and artists from the corps de ballet may be called upon to create a principal role in a new ballet, and there is a constant change in personnel as dancers are promoted or leave a company.

The term 'ballerina' is a vexed one; it implies both position in a company as a leading female dancer and a certain standard of attainment. It is not, as some daily papers would have us believe, the title for any girl who dances, but a recognition of status and achievement. In some companies it is still an official ranking – at the Paris Opéra the principal dancers are nominated as *étoiles*; in Imperial Russia there was only one prima ballerina assoluta, Mathilde Kshessinskaya (1872–1971). The title of ballerina that was hers, and is so rightly Margot Fonteyn's, is tarnished when it is applied to any dancer who hits the headlines.

The male dancer

Turning now to the men, it suffices to say that the standard of male dancing throughout the world has never been higher than it is today. This is a direct result of the fact that for the first time ever it has been possible for a man to take up dancing and have some guarantee of financial stability. The rewards are still not good enough (except, naturally, for a few great stars) and it is rare for dancers – male or female – to go on dancing after the age of forty. The male dancer in particular is faced with the terrible decision, especially if he has a family to support, as to what he shall do when he retires from dancing at an age when most men would think they are just in their prime. For women, the problem is also very considerable, but marriage and teaching opportunities do something to help the female performer to survive the end of a dancing career.

It is a curious fact that at the very beginnings of ballet in the court dances and spectacles of the sixteenth and seventeenth centuries the male was the dominant figure. By the end of the seventeenth century, ballet had entered the theatre. To begin with professional male dancers dominated the stage but in 1681 the first professional female dancers were seen in Paris. Although women, encumbered with heavy costume, did not dance such brilliant steps as the men for many years, by the end of the eighteenth century there was some measure of equality in technique between the sexes.

The nineteenth century sees the time when women become the more important figures in ballet. It is the time of the great ballerinas of the Romantic period (further details are given in Chapter Four). One of the worst results of the nineteenth century audiences' eagerness to see attractive girls was the fact that in some ballets (*Coppélia* for example) the boy's role was taken by a pretty girl who was not even meant to look and move like a man.

Nevertheless male technique did survive – notable in Italy, Denmark and Russia. It was with Diaghilev's company of Russian dancers at the beginning of this century that there came the re-awakening for ballet in Western Europe and the beginnings of a new awareness of male dancing.

During the twenty-five years after Diaghilev's death in 1929, while the national companies in England and America were being established without any financial help from governments, it was almost impossible for a male dancer to get the financial rewards that he deserved. There was also a prejudice in the public's mind that dancing was not a 'manly' profession – in spite of the fact that a male dancer had to be stronger, fitter and have greater stamina than the popular idols of the football field or the boxing ring. You have only to watch a male dancer lift a girl high above his head, with an ease that suggests she weighs nothing at all, and then carry her across the full width of the stage, to realize just what strength and effortless power is needed.

In two countries which had long established ballet traditions – Denmark and Russia – there was none of this prejudice. The men were helped also by the fact that dancers were state employees, in state companies, who could be sure of a pension when they retired. In Russia, of course, there has always been a marvellous tradition of folk dancing which has encouraged the men to show off in front of the more delicate female dancers with brilliant jumps and steps. Because of this, no one in Russia felt that is was unusual or effeminate for a man to dance.

Fortunately today the state companies in the West are now aware of the need to reward dancers more adequately, and the immense popularity of stars like Rudolf Nureyev, Edward Villella, and Anthony Dowell, to name only three of

Rudolf Nureyev as the Chief of the Polovtsian warriors in *Prince Igor*, a role in which Adolph Bolm astonished Paris with the Diaghilev Ballet in 1909.

many, has finally re-established the status of the male dancer. In fact, when a couple of outstanding dancers perform a 'party piece' like the dazzling *Don Quixote* pas de deux it is the male dancer who nearly always gets the loudest ovation.

The performance

The tremendously demanding day of the professional dancer has been described. It culminates in the performance in which all fatigue and worry has to be forgotten as the dancers seek to do their best. It is really only when the curtain falls that the dancer can relax, and eat the best and largest meal of the day. If you ever meet any dancers after a performance, never forget that they are starving hungry. They seldom eat before the show and all the energy that has been burned up on stage must be replenished as quickly as possible. The rich ladies who like to entertain ballet dancers at late-night parties have to realise that conversation and compliments must come *after* the dancers have been fed. Occasionally receptions are held for ballet companies at which all the food has been devoured by the other guests before the dancers had time to change and get there. Not surprisingly, parties like these are not a success. The dancers will say a few polite words and then leave, in search of much needed protein and a chance to unwind.

ROOTS

Like people, ballet companies are products of their home environment. Security and care, which are what we all look for in a home, are exactly what are found in the world's great ballet companies. Three things are needed above all else: a school to train the dancers and ensure that there is always fresh talent ready to be taken into the company; a choreographer – the person who actually composes the dances – to provide the new ballets that are needed each year to show off the dancers and also to give the company a 'personality'; and a home theatre in which the public knows that it will find the company for the greater part of the year.

In Britain
These three factors have always given stability to the world's finest ballets, and if we consider the history of Britain's Royal Ballet we can see that from the very beginning in 1931 Dame Ninette de Valois, who created the company, made sure that all these were available. Her company and school were first given a home at Sadler's Wells Theatre in North London, and during the formative years the school, the theatre and the choreographer – Sir Frederick Ashton – gave this troupe all the stability that was needed to turn it into a great national organization. In 1946 the Sadler's Wells Ballet was ready to move to the Royal Opera House, Covent Garden, and within a few years Dame Ninette also found residential premises to allow her school to expand. Nowadays The Royal Ballet, as Dame Ninette's company became, combines two ensembles and both a junior and a senior school. The company's official home is still the Royal Opera House, Covent Garden, which it shares with the Royal Opera, and it is one of the most charming theatres in the world. Its red and gold auditorium, seating more than

A remarkable, fish-eye lens view of the interior of the Royal Opera House, Covent Garden, which conveys something of the glamour and charm of one of the great opera houses of the world.

two thousand people, is over a hundred years old, as the portrait of the young Queen Victoria over the proscenium arch testifies. It is one of the most intimate theatres for ballet we know. Despite its size there is a feeling both welcoming and exciting as you sit waiting for the house lights to go down and the great red curtains to swing apart and reveal The Royal Ballet on its own ground. Backstage it is far less charming, with crowded dressing room conditions for the dancers, no rehearsal studios at all, and a warren of tiny offices and workrooms. Even so, it is a much loved theatre with its own tradition and a great sense of history about it.

What Dame Ninette achieved in London already existed in the world's oldest and finest companies. If they are taken in chronological order we must start with the ballet company of the Paris Opéra, which dates back almost to the very beginnings of ballet as we know it. We then move to Russia, to the great companies and schools in Leningrad and Moscow which were created in the eighteenth century. And from there to Copenhagen where the Royal Danish Ballet, which had also been founded in the eighteenth century, became really important during the middle of the nineteenth. It is important to note that these three oldest-established companies were all paid for and encouraged by the monarchy, so that the dancers in St Petersburg could refer to themselves as 'artists of His Imperial Majesty'. In England, the Royal accolade was not given until 1956, when the company had already achieved international fame by its own efforts. But, of course, there are few monarchs left in the world and none able to pay for a ballet company; ballet has always been expensive and now it is the state which usually foots the bill. Like owning a yacht, if one has to stop to wonder whether one can afford a ballet company, one can't!

In France
Although ballet was born in Italy in the fifteenth century, it was brought up and educated in France where dancing became a vital part of court entertainments – the fact that the King could 'star' in these reveals how much significance was attached to them. But by the end of the seventeenth century ballet had become properly established in the French theatre.Louis XIV had loved dancing and he founded an academy to encourage and improve the art, just as he had established other academies to concern themselves with music and language. In fact the Paris Opéra Ballet springs from the Académie Royale de Musique which Louis founded in 1671. For more than three hundred years there has been a continuity of teaching and performance that has triumphed over wars and Revolution and the burning of theatres.

The present Paris Opéra, the third theatre of that name, is a gorgeously elaborate building, just over a hundred years old, in the centre of Paris. It is full of staircases and statues and long promenades and mirrors. On state occasions, with its masses of chandeliers and members of the Garde Républicaine lining the staircases, it is very, very glamorous. At the opening of each season the ballet company is usually seen in a Grand Défilé. The whole depth of the stage is

As part of a Renaissance spectacle, this tremendously decorated barge was floated on the river Arno in the great festival of 1608, which was staged to celebrate the entry of the Archduchess Maria Maddelena into Florence.

revealed, right back to the *foyer de la danse* (the green room which is a big reception area behind the stage), and down this long vista of chandeliers the entire ballet company and the students from the school process to the front of the stage while the orchestra plays some stirring march or other. It is an immensely jolly occasion but it does also suggest one important thing about the Opéra, and that is the continuity and dignity of this living tradition of teaching and performance stretching back to the greatest days of French history. Unlike those at Covent Garden, the backstage facilities are ample; at the top of the building is the famous circular rehearsal studio called the *Rotonde* and from the very beginning the school has been an integral part of the theatre.

In Russia

In distant, barbaric Russia at the same time that Louis XIV was encouraging court ballet at his palace at Versailles, a crude attempt at court dancing was being made. Under Peter the Great (1672–1725) a first attempt was made to encourage social dance (from which ballet usually springs) at court. It was part of Peter the Great's policy to Westernize his country, to make his people aware of the outside world and to 'open a window on the West'. One stage in the opening of this window was to rid the boyars of their cumbersome robes; with lighter clothes they could dance more easily and they began to enjoy the polite forms of court dancing. (Russians, of every social class, have always loved and excelled at dancing.)

Within half a century of Peter's reforms the first dancing school had opened in St Petersburg and the Empress Anna had seen the first professional ballet in Russia in 1736. By the beginning of the nineteenth century ballet was firmly established under the protection of the Tsar. St Petersburg was the capital and became the true home of the Imperial Ballet, though companies were always maintained in Moscow and Warsaw (then part of the Russian Empire). During the nineteenth century the Imperial Russian Ballet owed almost everything to the influence of French and Italian choreographers, teachers and dancers. This influence culminated in the sixty years that the Frenchman Marius Petipa (1818–1910) spent in St Petersburg.

When ballet lost favour throughout the rest of Europe it remained enormously popular in Russia. Russian dancers became the finest in the world and masterpieces of ballet like *The Sleeping Beauty* were created which were to influence ballet the world over.

Russian ballet, which had learned so much from France, was to repay the debt in two ways. Firstly, several ballerinas fled Russia during the 1917 Revolution and eventually settled in Paris and, having lived off their jewels for some years, were forced to teach to earn a living and thereby hand on to several generations of dancers the great traditions of the Russian style.

The second repayment was even more considerable. By the beginning of this century ballet in the Imperial Theatres had become monumental and set in its ways. Even in an Opera House a ballet company must experiment or it will be overtaken by creeping paralysis. It fell to Serge Diaghilev (1872–1929) to show a new way for ballet to develop. His first incredible season in Paris in 1909 with new dancers, new ballets, new scenery and new music, was to set a pattern that made the Diaghilev Ballet Russe the most exciting artistic force in Europe for the next twenty years.

Diaghilev's company was forced to stay in the West by the Russian Revolution; after 1917 ballet in Russia had to change quite as much as did the whole way of life in the new Soviet Union. Instead of being 'artists of His Imperial Majesty' the dancers had to adapt to the socialist way of life. But ballet remained enormously popular. Indeed it became even more popular than ever before because the government, discovering in ballet a way of expressing the problems and ideals of a socialist state, encouraged everyone to attend. The old repertory still continued in the old theatres, although these changed their names. The Maryinsky Theatre in St Petersburg became the Kirov Theatre in Leningrad. New theatres were built all over the Soviet Union, and new ballet companies were started. A superb system of dance training was developed by the great teacher A Y Vaganova from her experience as a member of the old Imperial Ballet. Today the ballet companies of the Kirov Theatre and the Bolshoy Theatre are the wonder of the world. The young dancers of the Kirov company still practice in the same rehearsal rooms and studios that were known to Kshessinskaya, Pavlova and Nijinsky. The Maryinsky Theatre with its beautiful blue and silver auditorium is unchanged in all but name. The red and gold magnificence of the Bolshoy Theatre in Moscow has become even more important now that Moscow is the seat of government, and a massive new auditorium, the Palace of Congresses with 6,000 seats, has been built to house the vast new audience. Despite the tremendous and dreadful upheavals of the Revolution and the years which followed, the Russian ballet has survived and grown. It was firmly rooted: it had its great schools and theatres. It was because Diaghilev's Ballet Russe had no such roots that it could not survive his death.

In Denmark
Further proof of the importance of a school, a theatre and a choreographer is seen in the history of the Royal Danish Ballet. Like many other small nations in the eighteenth century, Denmark had its court ballet. But it was not until the nineteenth century that its ballet company achieved any real significance. This was due to the work of one man, August Bournonville, who had studied under the great French ballet teacher, Auguste Vestris in Paris. When he returned to Copenhagen in 1830 to become ballet master, choreographer and principal dancer he found himself in charge of a very feeble company which he had to revive and inspire. This he did, and what sustained his achievement and what has sustained the Royal Danish Ballet ever since, has been the system of training which he inherited and developed, as well as the profusion of fine ballets he created.

The Royal Danish Ballet was somewhat off the beaten track, so Bournonville's style and ballets were preserved almost unchanged. The school in which his teaching system reigned supreme, and the company which lived off the wonderful ballets he made, were untouched and lived almost in isolation until the 1950s when the Royal Danish Ballet ventured from Copenhagen and proceeded to delight the world.

The Royal Danish Ballet's home is the enchanting little Royal Theatre in the square half way between the Royal Palace and the waterfront. There are two stages: the traditional, nineteenth century Royal Theatre with its famous drop curtain with the motto 'Not for Pleasure Alone' – you are expected to take some of your theatre-going seriously – and the 'New Stage', a typically 1930s building which stands next door and is connected by a covered way above the street. The traditional repertory is nearly always shown in the older theatre. The New Stage is the home for the Royal Danish Ballet's wide-ranging modern repertory as well as for modern plays and pop musicals. The school is housed in the theatre. The

Gerda Karstens as the witch Madge and Poul Gnatt as James in the closing moments
of Bournonville's *La Sylphide*. Gerda Karstens was one of the most celebrated mime
artists with the Royal Danish Ballet, a company which has always boasted a tradition
of excellent and vivid miming.

ballet occupies the fourth floor, while the second and third are devoted to opera
and drama. Consequently there is a much closer relationship between artists
working on the three floors than happens in most state theatres.

In the USA

One other major company has grown up in recent years in rather the same way
that Britain's Royal Ballet has developed. This is the New York City Ballet,
where again the presence of a great choreographer and a fine school has made
possible the establishment of a classical ballet company with an American
accent. In 1933 Lincoln Kirstein, now Director of the company but at that time
not long out of Harvard, and his friend Edward M. M. Warburg, had the good
sense to invite George Balanchine to the United States. Their purpose was to
bring the classic ballet to America. Balanchine was a marvellous choice since he
was a product of the St Petersburg–Leningrad school and his ballets had already
shown great mastery of the classic dance. After many problems during the next
ten years they were given the chance to house their company at the New York
City Center in 1948. This was the starting point for the expansion of the NYCB,
now one of the finest companies in the world. The move to the City Center and
the acquisition of a home, prepared the way for the establishment of a permanent
ensemble which was fed by graduates from the company's school. The presence
of Balanchine, admired everywhere as the greatest choreographer of our time,
meant that the company had a clear and positive identity. In effect, Balanchine
made the classical ballet American and his output of ballets – over a hundred –
has shown that the academic dance can keep pace with even the most extreme
developments of modern music. In 1964, with the completion of the State
Theater in Lincoln Center (a vast arts complex in Central New York), NYCB
found a home worthy of its reputation.

The modern yet traditional State Theater represents a very positive
collaboration between the directors of the NYCB and the architect Philip
Johnson. It has a fine stage for dancing and the huge auditorium not only has
good sight lines but is also framed within a building that offers space and
elegance for audiences and for official receptions. As Lincoln Kirstein says,
'Performances do not take place only on stage; their rituals overflow into the
festive atmosphere of intermissions'. This is especially true on hot summer
evenings, when the audience can go out on to the balcony which overlooks the
fountains of Lincoln Center.

The spacious offices and rehearsal rooms of the NYCB are in the State

A view from the orchestra floor in the New York State Theater, Lincoln Center, home of the New York City Ballet. The theatre, which seats 2,729, has marvellous sight lines even from the top ring, no central aisle and ample leg room.

Theater, but the School of American Ballet is housed in the Juilliard School of Music building, across the Plaza. The school itself has a faculty which reads like a roll of honour of classic ballet in this century – its instructors include some of the greatest names from the old Maryinsky, from Copenhagen, and from England, as well as former dancers of the NYCB itself.

Around the world

Throughout the world the example, particularly of The Royal Ballet – one of the first national companies to tour abroad – has provided an inspiration for newer troupes. The success of the first Royal Ballet tour of the United States in 1949 inspired the Canadians to seek the foundation of a similar classical troupe. On Dame Ninette's advice Celia Franca, a distinguished English soloist, was invited to form one in 1951. After years of backbreaking work, financial crises and all the problems of pioneering, she created a classical company. It is sustained to a large extent by the excellence of its school (situated in Toronto and directed by Betty Oliphant), which ranks as one of the best in the world, with academic standards as high as its technical training.

Another Royal Ballet dancer, Peggy van Praagh, who had made an enormous contribution to the success of British ballet as director of the Sadler's Wells Theatre Ballet, was invited to Australia in 1962 to form a national company there. As in Canada, the presence of a school has been of great importance in guaranteeing the standards of the young and attractive Australian Ballet. Both these companies have made a point of staging the classic repertory as an essential part of their foundation.

Yet another Royal Ballet member, the late John Cranko, was able to benefit from his association with Dame Ninette when he was invited to direct the ballet company in Stuttgart in 1961. The establishment of a school was one of his first actions. With the advantage of his own choreographic gifts and the presence of a superlative ballerina in Marcia Haydee, the Stuttgart Ballet has not only won a devoted following in its home town within ten years but has also danced with great success in New York, Russia and London.

The few examples we have given of well-rooted companies suggest, we hope, the vital need for a school, a theatre and a choreographer. But this need for a secure base is also a matter of money, and in a later chapter we shall try and explain a few of the enormous complexities connected with balletic finance.

HOW
BALLETS
ARE
MADE

When the curtain goes up on the first night of a new ballet the aim of the dancers is to present something that looks easy, polished, and with none of the problems that have gone before still unsolved.

The audience must never know how far this impression is from the truth; the dancers' serene appearance is part of their craft. Behind the performance lie weeks and months of planning, worrying, disappointments, fits of temper and sleeplessness. The most curious thing about a first night is that no one – neither choreographer nor dancers nor director – has any real idea of what the finished product will be like. If a poet or a novelist is not satisfied with what he has written he can tear it up. An artist can paint over a canvas that does not please him. A composer can play through a work and alter and discard. In the cinema the director will see the 'rushes' every day and judge how successful the filming has been so far. In the straight theatre many major productions have previews in capital cities or are 'tried out' on tour before the official opening night. This means that sometimes for several weeks before the first night cuts and alterations can be made. Major ballet companies, on the other hand, who are resident in large theatres, simply cannot spare the time or the dancers for this luxury.

For a ballet company the first night is the occasion when all the components of steps, music and design are seen together for the first time. Not until then can the fruit of many months work by judged. Even the dress rehearsal is not a true picture of what is going to happen when the final component – the audience – is added.

A ballet comes into being for any one of several reasons. A choreographer may decide to make a work because he deeply wants to express certain ideas, but it is more likely that he will have to make it because the company he is working for needs a new piece in the repertory. Every company has to be fed with new works

Antony Tudor rehearsing Edward Villella and Patricia McBride of the New York City Ballet in a revival of his *Dim Lustre.*

as it is fed with new dancers. Dancers have to be developed in new roles. A choreographer may wish to explore the powers of a dancer he admires or show off a favourite dancer in a new way. In Germany, for instance, because of the demands of the audience, ballet companies have to provide two or three completely new programmes each season. In Britain, each season must include works new to the repertory of the company. In America both modern dance and classical ballet companies are obliged to whet their audiences' appetites with new works which will offer a contrast with the existing repertory.

Once he has decided upon the sort of ballet he has to make, the choreographer will then look around for a score. For the most part he has to listen to records until he finds the music which seems right for his purposes. He will do this in consultation with the company's music director or conductor, but occasionally he might hear a piece of music which so interests him that he determines to build a ballet on this basis. It is rare for a large company to commission scores, chiefly because composers need a considerable length of time to work on a new score (this is a point we shall discuss later). Sometimes a new score will be an arrangement of existing pieces. In such cases the style of a composer will have attracted the choreographer and then it is usually the musical director who will stitch together a patchwork of shorter pieces into a complete score. Two excellent surviving examples of this kind of arrangement are found in Constant Lambert's work for Sir Frederick Ashton. He arranged various Meyerbeer pieces for *Les Patineurs* and used Auber's music for *Les Rendezvous*.

Once the score has been decided upon, the choreographer can begin work. He usually goes in to rehearsal with some basic idea of what he wants to do; few choreographers face their dancers with any definite thoughts about the actual structure of the choreography, but consciously or unconsciously, they will be aware of the direction in which they want their ballet to go. A few choreographers – Marius Petipa, Dame Ninette de Valois are two well known examples – go in to rehearsal with a detailed and very clear understanding of what they intend to do, but this is an exception rather than the rule.

At this point we should digress for a moment to deal with the question of 'meaning'. If a choreographer makes a ballet which tells a story it is quite clear that the meaning will come across. But a great many ballets do not tell a story; they are plotless and are concerned perhaps with a mood or more often with showing quite simply the sort of movement that the music inspired in the choreographer's mind. Unfortunately when people go to the theatre to see a play or an opera they expect to be told something. Since they do not ask to be told anything by a symphony or a piano concerto, there is absolutely no reason why they should expect information from a ballet. As it was mentioned earlier, the great American choreographer Paul Taylor calls his ballets 'food for the eyes' and we would recommend the audience to view dancing in just this way. It is the movement that should please. If a choreographer wants to give messages or information he should write a play or send a telegram. Some of the most satisfying ballets may have a theme which inspired the original idea but this is not stated in precise terms. The audience is free to use its imagination and choreographers often prefer to give the audience this liberty of enjoyment.

Traditionally the choreographer begins work from the piano score. He does not necessarily begin at the beginning of the ballet, however. Sometimes he will start with a pas de deux, as both Sir Frederick Ashton and Kenneth MacMillan have done. Often he is obliged to make use of whatever dancers are free for rehearsal, and in a large repertory company these may well be dancers who do not appear until a late stage in the piece. (It must never be forgotten that dancers are first required to go to daily class and they also have to fit in the essential rehearsals which keep the company repertory at performance pitch.)

When rehearsals start for a new work, progress is never fast. The choreographer may spend a whole morning working with his dancers and yet

George Balanchine rehearsing Allegra Kent of the New York City Ballet.

produce barely one minute of finished choreography. On other mornings inspiration may flow more easily and a whole dance may be set. But it is idle to wait for 'inspiration'. As Sir Frederick Ashton said, 'if the Muse is there in the rehearsal room at ten in the morning, so much the better.' Like every choreographer, Ashton has learned that work must go on; time cannot be wasted and the choreographer's craft consists in being able to make steps whether he particularly feels like it or not. George Balanchine never ceases to remind his dancers that they are on 'Union time', and that time means money. Great choreography, of course, cannot be made to order, but much useful groundwork can be done on the 'grey' mornings.

While this daily work goes on, the choreographer has other concerns. He must be in consultation with both his designer and with the person responsible for the score, be it composer or arranger. The choice of the designer is entirely a personal one. The choreographer will often choose to work with an artist with whom he has collaborated happily in the past. There will already be an understanding between them, and in some cases the designer's ideas may well feed the choreographer's creativity.

Sometimes a choreographer may be attracted by the work of an artist seen in a gallery and will decide to take a chance on his ability to work in the theatre. An example of this is Robert Helpmann's choice of the distinguished easel painter Leslie Hurry to design his ballet *Hamlet* in 1942. This led on to Hurry's many distinguished contributions to the theatre as a designer. Theatre designing, like choreography, is a very special craft. It requires a most extensive knowledge not only of the possibilities of the stage but also of the unique requirements of clothes for dancing.

With his composer, the choreographer has to discuss the progress of the score, the possible need for cuts, certain dramatic requirements and the overall shape of the ballet. All the time he is hopefully piecing together the dances into the final structure. Some choreographers are ruthless with their own work. As the ballet is put together and long sections are run through, dissatisfaction with what he has composed may force a choreographer to discard the fruit of a week's work. Kenneth MacMillan had worked for three weeks on his *Rite of Spring* when he decided to start all over again. Maude Lloyd, a famous dancer who worked a great deal with Antony Tudor, told us that he left enough good choreography in the rehearsal room to make another ballet.

During the rehearsal period the choreographer is aware not only of his own s but also of the inspiration proffered by the bodies of his dancers. The or can find a very positive inspiration and challenge in a dancer's body and erament. He feeds upon the dancer's gifts, but these gifts also offer a lus. The choreographer has to explore and expand the dancer's abilities. As rting point he may ask a dancer to 'move from that corner of the room to ', or suggest a dramatic situation and ask the dancer to improvise. If the ancer has some knowledge of the choreographer's style, and if he trusts the dancer as a performer, a framework is established upon which the choreographer n elaborate. The dancer will present an idea for a movement which can become ined and shaped by the choreographer's own talent. In this way the soloist or incipal dancer can make a very real contribution to the final product, and sometimes on completion of a ballet no one is quite sure who thought of what. The finished work is, however, entirely the choreographer's own.

There have been several instances of this kind of inter-dependence of

---

Margot Fonteyn as Ondine and Michael Somes as Palemon in the Shadow Dance in the first act of Frederick Ashton's *Ondine*.

Lynn Seymour as Juliet in Kenneth MacMillan's *Romeo and Juliet*, in Act III in Friar Lawrence's cell; he has offered her the potion which will help simulate death and she faces the dreadful decision whether to take it.

choreographer and dancer. Notable examples in our time are the twenty-five year association between Frederick Ashton and Margot Fonteyn which began in 1935 with *Le Baiser de la Fée*, and the mutual enhancement of talents between John Cranko and Marcia Haydee, and between Kenneth MacMillan and Lynn Seymour. An extraordinary communication and empathy among such artists that has resulted in superb roles and superb ballets.

Design

During this whole period of creation the designer is ideally kept aware of all that is going on, and will be watching rehearsals. He will usually begin his work with the set. If the ballet is to be dramatic and literal he will have drafted an initial project for discussion with the choreographer, and nowadays will proceed to make a model of the set. When this has been agreed – obviously the location of doors, stage furniture or flights of stairs has to be settled early on – the designer will be much occupied with the actual building of his decor by the theatre's workshop, and lengthy consultations will take place in the paintshops with the people responsible for realizing the design. At the same time the designer will have drafted costume projects for discussion with the choreographer, and once these have been agreed on, work is put in hand in the theatre's wardrobe. Of prime consideration is the fact that dancers have to *move* and the costume must enhance that movement and in no way impede it. Fabrics have to be chosen with a sharp eye for their possibilities – it is pointless to weigh down dancers so that they cannot move – and most designers for ballet prefer to use natural rather than synthetic fabrics. The range of styles in ballet design is as great as the range of the ballet repertory, from the fairy-tale opulence of *The Sleeping Beauty* to the bare clarity of the black tights and white sweat shirts favoured by George Balanchine in many of his works.

Once the designs have been approved and decided upon, the making of the costumes begins. It is the task of the wardrobe staff to interpret the designs and, in discussion with the designer, to decide upon the cut and the fabrics to be used. Costumes can rarely, if ever, be true to life or even true examples of historical dress. Unlike the historical accuracy called for in the cinema or on television, it is an *illusion* of truth that is needed. An ordinary dress of today would look feeble on stage, and a literal re-creation of an historical costume would be completely unsuitable for dancing. The designer and the wardrobe department have to interpret in the light of the need for movement, and the need to stress certain elements to make them effective on the stage. In the same way that naturalistic gesture and movement has to be made theatrical by the choreographer, so too do all forms of costume and design.

Once the costume design has passed into the wardrobe, a very great deal of talent and skill is needed in the actual making of the garment. The wardrobe department must be able to create clothes from designs – there are no paper patterns – and the costumes must be so strongly made that no amount of physical exertion by the dancers will cause them to disintegrate. In addition it must never be forgotten that dancing is among the most arduous of physical activities and dancers sweat profusely. Costumes have to be able to stand up to being soaked with perspiration, to the constant cleaning that results, and to being worn by people who are moving fast and furiously. No matter how many times the white tarlatans have been worn in *Les Sylphides* they must always look pristine fresh to the audience. No hooks must wear loose; no shoulder straps may be insecure. Every detail has to be checked before every performance.

Two contrasting pictures of stage design. The Royal Ballet in the last act of *The Sleeping Beauty* as designed by Peter Farmer in 1973; and the New York City Ballet in George Balanchine's *Movements*, where stage decoration has been reduced to the minimum of leotards for the dancers.

Music

If a score is commissioned, the initial discussions between choreographer and composer are very lengthy if the work is to be a dramatic piece. In the nineteenth century the most celebrated example of this creative collaboration is that between Marius Petipa and Tchaikovsky. Petipa always provided his composer with a complete breakdown of the dramatic action of the full-length ballet. He would plan the whole work with the minutest attention to the effect he wanted to achieve and then go on to complete details of the number of bars of music required for each variation, the type of music, whether it was to be a Waltz or a March or a Mazurka, and sometimes even the actual orchestral sound. (For a complete study of this collaboration see *Ballet for All* by Peter Brinson and Clement Crisp, 1970.)

In recent years too, choreographers have sometimes offered very detailed guidance to their composers in the preparation of long dramatic ballets. Frederick Ashton provided the German composer Hans Werner Henze with complete notes when planning *Ondine*, and while Thea Musgrave was preparing *Beauty and the Beast* for the Scottish Ballet, she had lengthy discussions with both the choreographer, Peter Darrell, and the producer, Colin Graham. (Details of such collaborations are given in *Making a Ballet* by Mary Clarke and Clement Crisp, 1975.)

For plotless ballets, with their existing scores (there are rarely, if ever, commissioned compositions for this type of ballet), and for scores which are stitched together from existing music, problems of structure are easier to solve. But in working with any score there is one real difficulty in the rehearsal room. It has been traditional to work with a piano arrangement. The skill of the rehearsal pianist, accustomed to working with dancers, is considerable, but with the latest developments in modern music, problems arise, since it is all but impossible to reproduce the sound of the new orchestral sonorities, let alone electronic music, upon the rehearsal room piano. Some ballets have suffered because the difference between the sound of the piano 'reduction' and the full orchestra in performance is so great that it is almost unrecognizable to the dancers. Nadia Nerina has commented to us on the difficulty she found when she heard the full score of *Ondine* after working to a piano: she had to listen very intently to an orchestral recording of the score when preparing herself for the role, since many of the themes that had first guided her in rehearsal were lost in the full orchestral texture.

The contribution of the conductor is vital in any consideration of ballet in performance. He must not only know the score, he must also know the steps. He must guide the dancers in performance. Slack tempo will force dancers to break the flow of the choreography and result in a slack performance, whereas too quick a tempo will whip the dancers breathlessly round the stage, again destroy the choreography, and earn the conductor some very black looks from the performers. The best ballet conductors work as hard in rehearsal as do the dancers. Men like the late Yuri Fayer at the Bolshoy Theatre in Moscow and the

Dancers of the Alwin Nikolais company in *Tent*. This is an example of Nikolais' magical use of lighting and projections, with which he transforms both dancers and fabrics.

late Constant Lambert, who was the musical heart of The Royal Ballet during his lifetime, and today's Robert Irving of the New York City Ballet, and Ashley Lawrence of The Royal Ballet, know the steps almost as well as do the dancers. Consequently they know how to enhance both the dancers and the ballet.

Although throughout all the busy time of preparation, the choreographers, musicians and designers have been working in constant collaboration, their actual labours have taken place in different parts of the theatre. The choreographer and his dancers have been confined to the rehearsal studio – they do not see the stage until the first stage-call, which is usually a day or two before the dress rehearsal; the designer has been dashing between paintshops and wardrobe; the conductor has been rehearsing the orchestra elsewhere. Not until that first stage-call do all the pieces of the jigsaw finally come together on an agonizing morning when the ballet as such really sees the light of day for the first time. Problems of orchestration, disasters with the costumes (often unfinished and held together with safety pins), and impossible difficulties with the set, all have to be solved. Once the ballet is in the theatre another massive hurdle – the lighting – has to be taken. The importance of the lighting designer cannot be over-estimated. It is his task to bring the designs and the dancers to life. A good lighting man can make an indifferent ballet seem good, while bad lighting can ruin even the finest work. One of Diaghilev's most extraordinary gifts was to be able to give vitality to the works in his repertory by the most lengthy and painstaking preparation of stage lighting. It was the only thing he ever claimed to do for the Ballet Russe: 'You can say I do the lighting'. In his study of the Diaghilev Ballet, Boris Kochno, a poet and Diaghilev's right-hand man during the last six years of his life, records one of his first views of Diaghilev at work, spending a whole night labouring to light *Petrushka* and bringing the tired and battered old scenery to magical life.

Today lighting has become increasingly important in the dance theatre. Some ballets rely entirely for their decorative effects upon the lighting director, and excellence in this field is as rare as it is in choreography.

Then there comes the morning of the dress rehearsal on which the ballet is usually run through completely with orchestra, lighting and costumes. At the Royal Opera House, Covent Garden, the choreographer and his technical staff will sit in the Grand Tier armed with microphones, while various other members of the company and theatre staff watch from the stalls. Except in very special circumstances the ballet is run through completely while copious production notes are made of matters still to be ironed out before the first night. A short ballet will often be taken through twice. The first time the dancers will probably 'mark' (that is, just walk through the steps) rather than dance full out, so that they can be interrupted to have details put right. At the second run-through, the ballet is given in as near performance conditions as possible.

But even then the work is not complete. As was said earlier, the audience is missing. It is almost impossible to judge a comedy ballet if no one is out front laughing for instance. The dancers are aware of a dead auditorium; they cannot judge precisely where applause will come and how prolonged it will be. Frederick Ashton and the dancers of the Royal Ballet expected the dance for the cockerel and the chickens at the beginning of *La Fille mal Gardée* to be well received but they were astounded on the opening night when the number virtually stopped the show.

By the opening night the die has been cast. There, at last, is the ballet, the result of so much intensive work. Will the audience like it? Will the critics like it? The newspapers next morning, and then the box office, will provide the answers.

BALLETS
THEN

A look at ballet in the theatre today shows traces of its origins in the Rennaissance courts of Italy and in the French courts of the sixteenth and seventeenth centuries. These are only traces, however, and we can only guess at the style and manner of dancing then, but because dancing was an important activity in court life and because court life is well documented in pictures and in books we can hazard a reasonably informed guess at how the court ballet developed.

It is vital to understand that from the very beginning the court dances and court entertainments from which our ballet has grown were often 'political'. The early Italian dinner ballets of the fifteenth century were entertainments connected with great feasts given to celebrate a victory in battle or an important marriage or the accession of a new ruler in one of the Italian principalities.

These entertainments and the processions and displays which followed them were a combination of song and dance and music and elaborate scenic effects, all intended to show how important and splendid was the prince whom the entertainments glorified. Throughout Europe there developed a tradition of court festivities which could range from decorated barges on rivers to triumphal floats that were paraded both indoors and out. Especially popular were the occasions when many of the courtiers would tread through the measures of the social dances of the time. In a curious way these were very like the formation dancing that can be seen on television today in such programmes as *Come Dancing*: the main idea was to show floor patterns made by the performers. The difference was that dancing at court level involved the grandest and noblest of the land dressed in the height of fashion.

Court ballet was soon to be found throughout Europe, and dancing was an essential part of the courtier's education. It reached its culmination in the

A court ballet staged in the Salle du Palais Cardinal in Paris in the middle of the seventeenth century. As always at this time, the ballet was performed towards 'the presence'; in this case the young Louis XIV who is seen seated with his Prime Minister, Cardinal Mazarin.

French court of King Louis XIV where the King often took leading roles in these entertainments. Like others before and since, King Louis had a weight problem and in his early thirties he was obliged to give up exhibiting himself in this fashion. But his love for dancing continued and he had the good sense to foster the training of professional dancers who were now to take over from the noble amateurs as dance moved in to the theatre. It is at this time too that we learn that the five positions of the feet are an established fact in dance training. A vocabulary of movement had developed and the words for the steps survive unchanged in ballet classes of today – still in French.

The flowering of ballet in the eighteenth century was also the flowering of dance technique – though this is not yet like the technique we know today. The female dancer was much encumbered with long skirts and it was the male dancer who was the star performer. By the beginning of the next century, however, we can see the germ of the technique of today – a technique that was to owe a great deal to the increasing importance of the ballerina in the nineteenth century.

Marie Camargo dancing in about the year 1730. Because Camargo had learned to perform entrechat quatre she was quite determined to let the public see this, and accordingly shortened her skirts from ground length to mid-calf. This is one of the first attempts at liberating the female dancer from the cumbersome costumes of everyday life.

Ballets preserved*

For today's audiences the important date is 1832 and the appearance of Marie Taglioni in *La Sylphide*. This is the first of the Romantic ballets. Romanticism was an artistic movement which came into being in the years immediately following the upheaval brought about in Europe by the French Revolution, the Napoleonic wars, and the development of an industrial society in Europe. The 1820s and 1830s saw a great change in music, in painting and in the theatre. In ballet this meant a complete rejection of the classical and heroic themes that had hitherto been the favourite subject-matter. Even the style of dancing was to change following the example set by Marie Taglioni. With her grace and demure charm, her ethereal lightness and brilliant technique, Marie Taglioni became the embodiment of everything that the early Romantic ballet wanted.

---

* Because there are a great number of books which offer the 'stories of the ballets' we have not felt it necessary to give more than the barest outline of the action of some ballets. But we would also suggest that a performance will become very much more enjoyable if you have done your homework and have read up the story and something of the ballet's history before seeing it.

La Sylphide and the Romantic Movement

La Sylphide was staged at the Paris Opera in 1832 by Filippo Taglioni to exploit the unique and new gifts of his daughter Marie. Its story tells of a young Scotsman James on the eve of his marriage to Effie. A sylphide, a forest sprite, has fallen in love with him and so great are her charms that she manages to lure him away to the forest. He deserts Effie and in the second act we see him enraptured by the sylphide's grace as she dances for him in the forest. Alas, James had earlier offended an old witch Madge and she now takes her revenge by giving James a poisoned scarf which he in turn gives to the sylphide. This kills the forest sprite and she is borne away by her sister sylphides while James is left grieving and alone, having lost both his mortal bride and his supernatural love.

The ballet was an immediate and enormous triumph for Taglioni and for the whole idea of Romanticism in ballet which was concerned henceforth with the exotic, the strange and the mysterious.

Taglioni floated and bounded through the air and this image of grace and of brilliant technique has remained one of the greatest inspirations for ballerinas right up until today.

The Taglioni version of *La Sylphide* was lost, but another, that of August Bournonville, has survived. In 1836 he mounted a production in Copenhagen for his favourite pupil, seventeen year old Lucile Grahn, and this can still be seen in the repertories of many companies throughout the world.

Several other Bournonville works have been preserved in Copenhagen. Ballets such as *Napoli, La Ventana, Konservatoriet* (Bournonville's affectionate recreation of a Vestris class), and the universally popular divertissement from *Flower Festival in Genzano*, and it is in these that we get our best and truest view of the charm, strength and brilliance of a great Romantic choreographer. These ballets illustrate both Bournonville's stature as a choreographer – he was a master at inventing steps as well as dramatic action – and the enduring qualities of his training system.

His narrative ballets incorporate traditional mime, a language of gesture that has always been part of the dancers' art, but he also made use of natural, everyday gestures. Because of this, a tradition has grown up in Copenhagen that older dancers as well as actors and opera singers – members of the companies which share the Royal Theatre's stages – take mime roles in many of the old Bournonville ballets. Because they may be senior artists and do not look like dancers, there is a great feeling of truth and probability about their performances, and in a work like *Napoli* – a joyful story of Neapolitan fisher folk – the mime roles of a ballad singer and a macaroni seller are wonderfully true to life and enormous fun.

It is traditional now for Romantic ballets to be performed by female dancers on full pointe, but it is important to remember that dancing on the tips of the toes was neither common or really possible for any length of time during the Romantic era. Shoes were unblocked and were little more than lightweight coverings for the foot. It was not until later in the century, when stronger and blocked shoes were common, that virtuoso ballerinas were able to dance on pointe rather as they do today.

Inevitably productions have changed massively over the years – ballets have been expanded and developed by succeeding generations of producers and ballet masters. Similarly, the developments in female technique have meant that ballerinas have embroidered and expanded their roles and their way of dancing has become more open and more athletic. There is an enormous difference between the style of Marie Taglioni and that of Margot Fonteyn.

Giselle

The crown of the Romantic ballet was *Giselle*. Staged in 1841 at the Paris Opéra, this ballet was designed as a tribute to the remarkable talent of the young Carlotta Grisi. Born in Italy in 1819, she was discovered dancing in Naples in 1836 by Jules Perrot, one of the most celebrated male dancers of the time. He had left the Paris Opéra in 1835 to find greater opportunities for dancing elsewhere in Europe, and he felt that he had discovered in the young Carlotta a talent of great potential. He trained her and staged his first ballets for her. When the couple arrived in Paris in 1840 Carlotta made an immediate impression in an entertainment in a small theatre on the boulevards. At that time the Paris Opéra was without a star ballerina, as Taglioni was on tour in Russia and her great rival, the dramatic Fanny Elssler, had just left for America on a lengthy tour (which even included Cuba where her corps de ballet consisted of what she called superannuated cows, their dark skin liberally coated with white make up). The poet and balletomane Théophile Gautier fell in love with Carlotta and in order to facilitate her entry to the Opéra he devised the libretto of *Giselle* for her. He had been inspired by a book of German folk tales. The story dealt with a simple village girl in medieval Germany who loves and is loved by a dashing young man whom she knows as Loys. She is also loved by a gamekeeper called Hilarion who is suspicious of Loys – with good reason. The young man is in fact a nobleman, Count Albrecht, masquerading as a peasant so that he can court Giselle. The arrival of the Duke of Courland and his daughter Bathilde who are hunting in the local forests, bring about the revelation of Loys' true identity and the fact that he is betrothed to Bathilde. This news so distresses Giselle that she becomes mad and in the most celebrated scene of the first act of the ballet we see her dance in delirium the steps she had danced so happily with Loys, and fall dead at his feet. The second act brings to the stage the legend of the Wilis that had first interested Gautier. The Wilis are young girls who have been betrayed and died for love; at night, they rise from their graves and dance to death any man they encounter.

The Pas de Déesses (The Judgement of Paris) in London in 1846, with Arthur St Léon surrounded by three of the greatest stars of the time, Marie Taglioni, Lucile Grahn and Fanny Cerrito.

When Albrecht comes, full of remorse, to lay flowers at Giselle's grave in the forest, the ghost of Giselle appears, still tenderly in love with him. But she is now a Wili and is commanded by the Queen of the Wilis to join in dancing Albrecht to death. Giselle does everything she can to sustain him during this ordeal and in the end she succeeds as the first rays of the morning sun destroy the Wilis' power. As the Wilis melt away and Giselle leaves Albrecht for ever, we see that although exhausted, he is still alive.

The ballet was officially to be choreographed by Jean Coralli the Opéra's ballet master, but Jules Perrot was responsible for all the dances for Giselle and Albrecht, roles created by Carlotta Grisi and Lucien Petipa. Perrot's understanding of Carlotta's gifts meant that the role was perfectly tailored to her abilities. The ballet and her performance were an absolute triumph. The role of Giselle was assumed by many other stars of that time, notably the Austrian-born dancer Fanny Elssler. The ballet was seen all over Europe and in America, but it survived really through its popularity in St Petersburg. It remains the single greatest creation of the Romantic Ballet.

Perrot was accorded little success in Paris, but in 1842 he came to London for six years and mounted a series of productions that are acknowledged as some of the finest achievements of the Romantic ballet. One of his productions included the legendary divertissement *The Pas de Quatre* which was designed to show off no fewer than four of the greatest female dancers – Taglioni, Grisi, Fanny Cerrito and Lucile Grahn.

Queen Victoria loved this sort of entertainment and the charms of the foreign virtuosi. But the Romantic works were designed to show off only the female stars while male dancers were almost completely ignored. It is significant that as this happened, ballet lost some of its vigour and popularity in the West. Like all others, theatrical fashions change, and ballet underwent a decline in the West. It became little more than a poor relation found in operas and music halls as incidental dances. But under the patronage of the Tsar, ballet continued to flourish in Russia, and it is there that the story of ballet really continues.

Jules Perrot went to St Petersburg in 1849 and for the next ten years he staged a series of ballets that displayed the talents of dancers like Elssler, Grisi and Grahn, but also helped to form a generation of Russian ballerinas that emerged from the well established ballet schools of Imperial Russia. When Perrot left Russia he was succeeded as chief ballet master by another Frenchman, Arthur St Léon. He was famous as dancer, choreographer, and violinist and when he went to Russia he was expected to choreograph dances for himself in which he also played the violin.

Coppélia

From 1860–69 St Léon commuted every year between Petersburg and Paris, producing a considerable number of ballets in both countries. In 1869 he left Russia for the last time and on his return to Paris he completed the staging of what was to be his last ballet, *Coppélia*. Despite the fact that it is one of the happiest of all ballets it had a tragic history when first performed. It starred a beautiful young Italian girl, Giuseppina Bozzacchi, who had been chosen at the age of sixteen to take the leading role of Swanilda, and who justified every hope by giving a most appealing portrayal of the naughty, charming heroine. But a couple of months after the ballet was staged the Franco-Prussian war of 1870 broke out, and France was to suffer terrible privations. Bozzacchi fell ill and died within six months. In the autumn of 1870 St Léon himself died; soon afterwards the original interpreter of the role of Dr Coppélius also died. But the ballet itself has survived. At the end of the Franco-Prussian war it returned to the Paris Opéra and was staged in St Petersburg where it was performed with different choreography. The story is appealing. It tells of Franz who falls in love with a mechanical doll (the Coppélia of the title) and his girl-friend Swanilda who finally manages to rescue him from enchantment. The score by Léo Delibes is an absolute delight.

Marius Petipa, another Frenchman, followed St Léon as chief ballet master in St Petersburg. He had gone to Russia as a dancer but had also helped Perrot with his productions. Under Petipa's rule, which lasted more than forty years, ballet entered its greatest period in Imperial Russia. Ballet training flourished and became the finest in the world, and a truly Russian style was developed.

The Sleeping Beauty
The ballet companies in St Petersburg and Moscow were part of the Tsar's household and every year Petipa was required to stage a new ballet. He started a tradition of long and complex ballets, often with very silly stories (which can be read in Cyril Beaumont's *Complete Book of Ballets*) but always full of superb dancing. These complicated spectacles reached their zenith in *The Sleeping Beauty* which he staged in 1889–90. The well known fairy story was the basis for four spectacular acts which made use of the massive resources of the great company and a great school. The guest ballerinas were often Italians – the training from the Milan ballet school, which was based on the teachings of a great pedagogue Carlo Blasis (1797–1878), gave them greater technical virtuosity than the local Russian dancers – but home grown ballerinas were soon to rival the Italians. When he came to create *The Sleeping Beauty* Petipa was already seventy-one years old, but the magnificence of the score Tchaikovsky wrote for him* seems to have given Petipa fresh inspiration, even though he was very set in his ways by then. The score was immensely superior to the pedestrian tunes that were produced to order by men like Ludwig Minkus, who held the official position of 'composer to the Imperial Ballet'. *The Sleeping Beauty* was Petipa's masterpiece. It is a cascade of wonderfully made dances, from the fairy variations of the Prologue (each one a jewel and each demanding at least a leading soloist if not a ballerina to do it justice), through the great pas d'action of the Rose Adagio, to the complete contrast of the Vision Scene, culminating in the virtuosity of the last act. The role of the Princess Aurora is the greatest testing piece in the classical repertory.

---

* For details of the remarkable collaboration between Petipa and Tchaikovsky see *Making a Ballet* by Mary Clarke and Clement Crisp (Studio Vista).

The Nutcracker

The success of *The Sleeping Beauty* meant that the Imperial Ballet asked Tchaikovsky for another score, and Petipa proposed a two act ballet called *The Nutcracker*. Tchaikovsky completed a score as Petipa asked for it but the old ballet master fell ill and the work was in fact choreographed by his assistant, the Russian Lev Ivanov.

Ivanov was a very different sort of man from the precise and careful Petipa. He was something of a romantic and in the snowflake scene and the pas de deux of the second act in *The Nutcracker* he showed himself to be very in tune with Tchaikovsky's luscious music. Sadly, the staging of *The Nutcracker* was not a success because the dramatic story is so weak and the role for the ballerina hardly worthwhile – she has only one pas de deux to dance.

Swan Lake

The year after *The Nutcracker* was staged in St Petersburg Tchaikovsky died. The Imperial Ballet decided to honour his memory by a memorial performance which would make use of a ballet score he had composed sixteen years previously for the Moscow ballet. This was *Swan Lake*, which had been a disastrous failure in all its three Moscow stagings between 1877 and 1882. Now in 1894 Ivanov choreographed the second act and the beauty of this lakeside scene was such that it was decided to stage the whole ballet. Ivanov was responsible for Acts II and IV, while Petipa choreographed Acts I and III. Thus the most popular of all ballets was launched.

The story of Prince Siegfried who meets his true love in the enchanted swan princess Odette surely needs no re-telling. What is important is the magnificence of the Petipa and Ivanov choreography – all the more important today when so many companies and choreographers decide to try to improve on the original and always fail dismally. The double role of Odette the swan queen and Odile the enchanter's daughter who deceives Siegfried is a wonderful one for the ballerina. The dances in these two roles are totally different but complementary – the ballerina must be both lyrical and dazzling.

Swan Lake is the most popular ballet in the world today. It has been in continuous performance since it was first staged. Like many others of the 'classics' it has been altered and revised by producers and ballet masters throughout the world and ballerinas of all types have been seen in the double role of Odette-Odile. This will suggest to you the fact that dancers often have considerable freedom in the way in which they perform a role. They are expected of course to respect the existing choreography but just as no two Hamlets are the

The closing moments of *Swan Lake* **as performed by The Royal Ballet. Rothbart's spell has been broken and Odette and Siegfried have been united in the kingdom under the sea.**

same (although they speak the same words) the different training, different bodies and different temperaments of the ballerinas mean that no two interpretations of Odette-Odile are the same. The subtle differences lend constant freshness to the ballet.

Although it was producing great dancers and great ballets, the Imperial ballet was becoming set in its ways. The court audience who had to be pleased by the ballet was very stuffy in its taste. The old generals and important civil servants who filled the front rows of the Maryinsky Theatre stalls and the Grand Dukes and aristocrats in the boxes who took the closest possible interest in the female dancers, all wanted to see pretty girls, wearing the jewels they had given them, displaying a neat pair of legs in pirouettes and arabesques. There was inevitably a reaction against this state of affairs and eventually this was to take the form of the Diaghilev Ballet Russe.

Serge Diaghilev (1872–1929) had had no practical link with ballet. He made his name as a young man in the world of painting as a promoter of exhibitions. With a group of friends which included the artists Alexandre Benois and Leon Bakst, he was in the forefront of new ideas about the arts in Russia. During the 1900s he promoted concerts and an operatic season of Russian music in Paris, and in 1909 he organized a combined opera and ballet season there. But it was impossible to show the wonderful new generation of dancers – they included Pavlova, Karsavina and Nijinsky – in the cumbersome Petipa repertory. Fortunately he found in Mikhail Fokine, a young choreographer and dancer who was already making a name for himself as the apostle of a new style of ballet, more truthful and more poetic than the standard Maryinsky repertory, the ideal creator of works to show off the dancers.

For the first Paris season of the Diaghilev Ballet Russe, Fokine's ballets *Les Sylphides, Le Pavillon d'Armide, Prince Igor* and *Cléopâtre* were danced by a group of artists on summer leave from the Imperial theatres. *Les Sylphides* won an audience straight away. Fokine made it as an evocation of the world of the Romantic Ballet and, especially of the graceful figure of Marie Taglioni drifting through the night air in *La Sylphide*. It is a reverie in which a youth is seen dancing in company with a host of sylphides, their long white dresses gleaming in the moonlight. The ballets were not all new; what was new was the excellence of the design and, for Paris, the amazing skills of the dancers.

Pavlova, Karsavina, Nijinsky and Bolm were a revelation. Ballet was suddenly reborn in the West and from the success of the first season there came the plan for a visit the next year which brought two new particularly significant works, both by Fokine. The first, *Schéhérazade*, an oriental fantasy inspired by a story from the Arabian Nights, dazzled the world with the colouring of Bakst's designs; they brought about a revolution in stage design. The second, *The Firebird*, a fairy tale about a young prince who is helped by the magic firebird to rescue an enchanted princess from the spells of an evil magician, introduced the greatest ballet composer of the century, Igor Stravinsky.

With success like this, and with the highest artistic ideals, there came the establishment of a permanent company under Diaghilev. Until his death in 1929 the Ballet Russe remained the foremost ballet company in the west. Though some artists left him, Diaghilev contrived to replace them with fresh talents. Fokine left finally in 1914, but by then he had produced a series of magnificent works including *Petrushka*, his supreme masterpiece. Fokine's choreography, Benois' designs and Stravinsky's music had all been created simultaneously for this ballet. It is the story of three puppets at a winter fair in St Petersburg in 1840. Petrushka himself, a role created by Nijinsky, is a tragic figure, as within the sawdust of his body there is a glimmer of a soul.

Nijinsky was encouraged to become a choreographer and his three works which were supervised by Diaghilev, *L'Après-midi d'un faune*, *Jeux* and *Le Sacre du printemps*, indicated a completely new view of what dancing could be, a rejection of classic vocabulary for a way of moving that contained many modern ideas.

As Lincoln Kirstein has said: 'Each one was of capital importance; each one meant an attack on a root element of dancing; *Faune*, the walk as (also) dance; *Jeux*, psychological material as suitable for academic dancing; *Le Sacre*, new uses of the whole corps de ballet as a single element; three really novel statements'.

When Nijinsky was dismissed, Diaghilev found a new young leading dancer in Leonide Massine. Even during the appalling hardships that the Ballet Russe knew during the first world war, Massine was educated and encouraged to become a choreographer so that by the end of the war, when the Diaghilev Ballet *left* The Royal Ballet's staging of *Petrushka*, in 1957 shows Alexander Grant as the tragic puppet dying in the last scene. The production was a meticulous recreation of one of the greatest of the Diaghilev ballets.

The Royal Ballet in Nijinska's *Les Noces*, revived by the choreographer in 1966.

returned to London, Massine was revealed as a major choreographer. By then, at the age of twenty-four, he had created *The Good Humoured Ladies, La Boutique Fantasque* and *The Three Cornered Hat. The Three Cornered Hat* had a score by Falla and designs by Picasso. Despite great financial problems and being cut off from Russia as a result of the Revolution, Diaghilev continued his ceaseless quest for the new and exciting in ballet.

He discovered painters, composers, dancers and he launched an extraordinary number of creative artists. His company's achievement in every aspect of ballet was remarkable and its range still astonishes us. Whatever the troubles of the 1920s, the Diaghilev company continued producing ballets that even today are important and significant. In 1923 *Les Noces* was staged. It was choreographed by Nijinsky's sister Bronislava Nijinska to a Stravinsky score. When it was revived by Nijinska for Britain's Royal Ballet in 1966 *Les Noces* still had the power to astound us by its modernity.

In 1924 the young dancer and choreographer George Balanchine fled Leningrad with a group of dancers who soon joined the Diaghilev troupe. Balanchine was soon recognized as a choreographer of genius and his two last works for Diaghilev, *Apollo* in 1928 and *The Prodigal Son* in 1929, survive to this day in the repertory of many companies as testimony to the early flowering of his great talent.

Diaghilev was always obsessed with youth. He favoured young dancers, making them stars when they were barely in their twenties; young composers and young designers found in him a director eager to make use of their ideas. It was because of the youth of his entourage up to the very last days of his life that so many of his collaborators are still influential in today's ballet.

BALLETS NOW

If we look at the repertory of Britain's Royal Ballet, we are also looking at its history – there are works still in performance which date from the beginnings of the company. Lovely jokes like *Façade* have survived for more than forty years and Ashton's *Les Rendezvous* is also a reminder of early days, when Alicia Markova was the ballerina to whom Ninette de Valois turned to appear in many of her stagings. Also the fact that The Royal Ballet today still performs *Swan Lake, The Sleeping Beauty, Giselle* and *Coppélia* is a reminder that from the start, Dame Ninette knew these nineteenth century works were very important both for her dancers and for her audience. Like Shakespeare and Sheridan in the theatre, or Mozart and Verdi in the opera house, they are the classics from which so much later development has sprung. The principal roles in the classic ballets – like the great roles in Shakespeare and in opera – are a touchstone for excellence. These roles give opportunities to the public to judge the qualities of the dancers, and to the dancers to display their own dramatic and physical skills while performing set choreography.

If the nineteenth century survivals form the base of most classical repertories, they are only a foundation on which everything else has to be built. Every company must find new choreographers to enrich the repertory constantly. Unlike drama and opera, ballet has only a tiny classical repertory from which to draw. With a company like The Royal Ballet it has also been an important part of company policy over the years to revive and preserve the most important ballets from the twenty glorious years of the Diaghilev Ballet Russe. In recent years, the London Festival Ballet and the Joffrey City Center Ballet in New York have also made use of this great heritage.

Of Diaghilev's early production, Fokine's *Les Sylphides* still survives. It is a ballet of mood, sometimes happy, sometimes nostalgic, but always extremely difficult to perform well because it demands so much more than technique. The ghosts of Pavlova, Karsavina and Nijinsky still haunt the work, and the dancers of today have the awe-inspiring task of living up to the legends. Fokine's two famous exotic works, *The Firebird* and *Schéhérazade* and his masterpiece *Petrushka* are also still performed. In 1954 *The Firebird* was revived by The Royal Ballet to celebrate the twenty-fifth anniversary of Diaghilev's death. Dame Margot Fonteyn was taught the title role by Karsavina, and a great deal of Karsavina's magical presence can be recognized in Fonteyn's performance. By being passed on from one interpreter to another in this way, some of the great roles in ballet are preserved. From Diaghilev's later repertory Massine's *La Boutique Fantasque* and *The Three Cornered Hat* have survived. And Massine's *Parade* has been revived by both the Joffrey and the Festival Ballets, although the interest today is primarily in the Picasso designs.

When Sir Frederick Ashton became Director of The Royal Ballet in 1964, he paid tribute to his one-time teacher, Bronislava Nijinska, by inviting her to stage for the company two of the finest works she had choreographed for the Ballet Russe, *Les Biches* and *Les Noces*.

Diaghilev's final choreographer was George Balanchine and The Royal Ballet, like Balanchine's own wonderful New York City Ballet, preserves his two finest works from this time: *Apollo*, a masterpiece of modern classical dancing, and *The Prodigal Son*, which tells the Biblical parable in vivid terms.

British choreographers

The opulent staging of many ballets today is made possible by that ingredient which plays such a vital and worrying part in the running of all companies – a sufficiency of money. In the 1930s, when the great British and American companies of today were in their infancy, money was very short indeed but, both in Britain and in America, there were young choreographers creating ballets. Far more important than money, for the health of any ballet company is that its school and its choreographer should be productive, and even in the earliest days of the Vic-Wells (now Royal) Ballet these ingredients were present.

During the 1930s Dame Ninette de Valois herself created many ballets and she was soon to invite Frederick Ashton to join her. Of Dame Ninette's own ballets three major works survive from this time. *Job* is a masque telling the Old Testament story of Job and his afflictions; *The Rake's Progress* is a lusty drama, inspired by four paintings by the eighteenth century English painter William Hogarth, which tell how a young man dissipates his fortune and dies in a madhouse; and *Checkmate* is a ballet inspired by the game of chess, in which the evil black pieces triumph over the red.

But it is to Sir Frederick Ashton that we turn for the great contribution to the building of an English style of classical dancing. For thirty years his ballets have helped more than anything else to make the company, its repertory and its dancers some of the greatest in the world. He has used and developed the English

Ninette de Valois' *The Rake's Progress*. Robert Helpmann as the Rake, enjoying himself immensely in a brothel, where Gerd Larsen has just rolled down her red stockings.

dancers' feeling for music and he has encouraged them to be sensitive in dramatic expression: foreign observers are often amazed at English dancers' acting ability and the way it is fused with a lyric style of movement.

Throughout most of this time he collaborated with Dame Margot Fonteyn, who epitomizes the English ballerina. In lyric ballets like the plotless *Symphonic Variations*, in dramatic works like *Marguerite and Armand*, and in comedy like *A Wedding Bouquet*, Ashton has made a permanent contribution to the public's enjoyment of ballet. He has shown how the full length ballet can still hold an audience in works such as *Cinderella* and *Ondine*, made for Fonteyn, *The Two Pigeons* for Lynn Seymour and Christopher Gable, and *La Fille mal Gardée*, inspired by the virtuosos Nerina, Blair, Grant and Holden.

It is impossible to do full justice to Sir Frederick's genius in a short book (David Vaughan's biography will do the task for us) and in any case his ballets can be seen wherever The Royal Ballet appears. But for the newcomer to ballet, we can unreservedly recommend *La Fille mal Gardée* as an ideal introduction. It is the happiest, brightest and most touching example of choreography that we know. And not to have experienced the feeling of delight as the cockerel and the hens start their capers at the beginning of the ballet is to have missed one of the nicest things in the whole of the theatre. Even the most prejudiced ballet haters have been won over by *Fille*, which glows like sunshine as the naughty Lise tricks her mother and wins the boy she loves. The mother is a role always danced by a man, in the English pantomime tradition, and it contains an irresistible and very funny clog dance. Ashton also included a mime sequence taught to him by Karsavina who had performed it in St Petersburg fifty years before. Ashton so loved the idea of this old fashioned mime, in which Lise dreams of marriage and of bringing up her children that he incorporated it in his new staging. For good measure, *Fille* also contains a Maypole dance, a real pony, a marvellous comic simpleton who flies into the air in a storm, and a red umbrella.

Dame Ninette and Sir Frederick established a tradition of English choreography in The Royal Ballet which was continued by the next generation, John Cranko and Kenneth MacMillan. John Cranko came to London in 1946 from South Africa and quickly revealed a wonderful talent for dramatic choreography and especially for comedy. In the English repertory his *Pineapple Poll* is a perennial favourite; and the very important collection of ballets he staged in Stuttgart from 1960 until his early death in 1973, have been acclaimed throughout the world. These include several ballets inspired by literature. The tragic *Onegin*, based on Pushkin's poem, and the joyous *Taming of the Shrew*, a version of Shakespeare's play, are among the most successful. Like Ashton with Fonteyn, Cranko was inspired by his ballerina, the Brazilian Marcia Haydee, a magnificent artist, and also by two of his male dancers, the American Richard Cragun and the Dane Egon Madsen.

Kenneth MacMillan, now Director of The Royal Ballet, was a contemporary and friend of Cranko's. He graduated from The Royal Ballet school to become a soloist, and was a very fine classical dancer. He began to choreograph ballets in

Nadia Nerina as Lise in the mime scene in the second act of *La Fille mal Gardée*, seen here imagining one of her babies behaving naughtily. A surprise is in store for her, not unconnected with the stooks of corn behind.

the 1950s and has produced over twenty works for the repertory since then. Among the most important are *The Rite of Spring*, a tribal ritual; *The Invitation*, a tragedy about a young girl; *The Song of the Earth*, an interpretation of a symphony by Mahler; and recently two show pieces for the company, *Elite Syncopations* with its ragtime score by Scott Joplin and others, and *The Four Seasons*, a cascade of brilliant dances that show off the present strength of The Royal Ballet.

MacMillan has also produced three full-length works that continue the Petipa/Ashton manner. *Romeo and Juliet* is a version of Shakespeare's play danced to the superb Prokofiev score. *Anastasia* is about the mysterious figure of Madame Anna Anderson, who claims to be the Grand Duchess Anastasia, sole survivor of the murdered Russian Imperial family. It portrays the young Anastasia and then the sufferings of Anna Anderson in her fight to establish her identity. Both these ballets were inspired by the great talents of Lynn Seymour. MacMillan's third full-length ballet is *Manon*, adapted from a French eighteenth century novel and first danced by Antoinette Sibley, Anthony Dowell and David Wall.

At the same time as Dame Ninette de Valois was building her company at Sadler's Wells Theatre, Dame Marie Rambert (a Polish dancer who had worked briefly with Diaghilev and had married the English playwright Ashley Dukes), started a school in London. From this developed the tiny but immensely important Ballet Club which gave performances during the 1930s. Rambert's talent lay in the discovery and encouragement of young artists. It was she who launched Ashton and also discovered another remarkably gifted choreographer, Antony Tudor.

The Ballet Club was fashionable, and professional in its standards and in its performers. Although it could only give limited seasons, and these usually in the minute Mercury Theatre in Notting Hill Gate, the Ballet Club staged Tudor's first ballets and two of them, *Jardin aux Lilas* and *Dark Elegies*, are still preserved in the repertories of several companies. *Jardin aux Lilas* explores the emotions of a girl forced to marry a man she does not love, who bids farewell to her beloved at an evening party in a garden filled with lilac bushes. *Dark Elegies* is inspired by Gustav Mahler's 'Songs on the Death of Children'; it is a sombre portrait of a group of parents who mourn the loss of their children.

When, in the late 1930s, Tudor left Rambert to work with his own company and then to go to America (where he has been based ever since), Dame Marie demonstrated her remarkable ability to discover new choreographers. Creators such as Andrée Howard, Walter Gore, and Frank Staff enriched the repertory. But in the post-war years, the Ballet Rambert fell victim to the demands of provincial audiences for classic ballets or ballets with familiar names. Presenting the classics demands a large company and this was alien to the Ballet Rambert's identity. Their admirable productions of *Giselle* and *La Sylphide* were joined by less admirable companions. Although Dame Marie found another choreographer Norman Morrice, whose first ballet, *The Two Brothers*, was produced in 1950, her company became financially trapped into producing classics for the provinces. 1966 was a year of crisis for both the Rambert and the Festival Ballet and financial troubles nearly destroyed them both; but the Arts Council of Great Britain stepped in and encouraged Dame Marie and Norman Morrice to reshape the company entirely. It became a group of soloists, with a repertory of largely contemporary works. Morrice's own taste for more modern movement, and the example of Nederlands Dans Theater – a very adventurous Dutch group – helped to transform the Ballet Rambert.

The American choreographer Glen Tetley had worked for Nederlands Dans Theater and he was invited to contribute works to the Ballet Rambert repertory. His first success for Rambert – and indeed his first created ballet – was *Pierrot Lunaire*. First staged in New York in 1962, it entered the Rambert repertory in 1967. The ballet has only three characters; the Pierrot of the title, tormented by Columbine whom he loves and by Brighella, a brigand-like figure who tries to dominate him. The setting by Rouben Ter-Arutunian is a white tower made of scaffolding. The costumes – Pierrot in white, Brighella in black and dark green, and Columbine in glorious crimson and white – make a stunning stage picture. The action of the ballet shows how Pierrot, simple, innocent, forgiving, learns to accept his tormentors. Christopher Bruce's performance in the title role is one of the most exceptional interpretations in British ballet. He has been acclaimed as one of the most outstanding actor-dancers of our time, and it is typical of the achievements of the new Rambert company that he should be encouraged also to choreograph.

With Norman Morrice and Glen Tetley contributing major works to the repertory and with dancers from the company – like Bruce – also beginning to make new works, the Ballet Rambert of the early 1970s became a most creative company. The style of dancing showed how classical ballets could be strongly influenced by contemporary dance. The Rambert girls were rarely seen on pointe, although the company still did classes in classical as well as in contemporary dance technique.

Modern dance had begun in the United States at the beginning of this century as a protest against the artificiality of classical ballet. Inspired by the example of Isadora Duncan, that great and unhappy woman, modern dance itself was given

Glen Tetley's *Pierrot Lunaire*, re-staged for the Ballet Rambert in 1967. Christopher Bruce in the title role is seen here with Gayrie MacSween as Columbine.

its first impetus by the dancing and teaching of Ruth St Denis and Ted Shawn. From their school and company came the two most important figures, Martha Graham and Doris Humphrey, as choreographers and teachers. From these two stem most of the tremendous vitality of modern dance throughout the world today. The fundamental difference from classical ballet lies in modern dance's acceptance of the force of gravity. For classical ballet often means an attempt at flight, at leaping away from the earth with maximum ease and grace. Modern dance is rooted in the earth. It also makes use of the breathing rhythms of the body, and 'contractions' and 'releases' are among the basic exercises. It was performed barefoot, in opposition to classical ballet's constricting slippers.

The demands of modern dance are as searching in their way as those of classical ballet, but it is possible to start a career as a modern dancer rather later (in the late teens and early twenties). This means, of course, that although a classical dancer can undertake modern dance roles, it is impossible for a dancer trained solely in modern dance to perform in the classical style. The great differences and rivalries that once existed between the two ways of dancing are rapidly giving way to a respect and interest in each others' methods, and it is remarkable how they have started to affect each other in recent years.

In the late 1960s the teaching system of the celebrated Martha Graham was brought to London. Graham had appeared with her company in Britain during the 1950s and 1960s and Robin Howard, an hotel owner with a passion for dance, made funds available for the establishment of a school to teach her method. With Graham's encouragement, and with members of her company as teachers, the London School of Contemporary Dance was founded in 1967. At first it was dependent on American skills but gradually a clearly British style evolved. However, the London Contemporary Dance Theatre, the company which grew out of the school, owes much to the guidance and to the choreography of Robert Cohan, formerly a principal dancer with the Graham company.

Cohan has made many works for the repertory, but the most popular is his full-length work, *Stages*, a multi-media exercise which has stimulated excitement among the young audiences who now find such pleasure in the offerings of modern ballet companies. By 1975 the LCDT had not only produced a British style of modern movement but also several interesting young choreographers, including Richard Alston, Robert North and Siobhan Davies.

Interestingly, the London Festival Ballet, a company diametrically opposed to it in style, found a young choreographer from the LCDT, Barry Moreland. He had made several works at The Place (LCDT's home theatre in London) and when he joined Festival Ballet he choreographed a very popular and effective Ragtime ballet, the two-act *Prodigal Son*. Danced to Scott Joplin music, this ballet tells the story of a young man journeying through the twentieth century, tap-dancing his way through Ragtime, the Depression and two world wars, always a victim but eventually triumphant. Despite its title, the ballet is more like a contemporary 'Everyman' than the Biblical parable. For the most part, however, the Festival Ballet's repertory has featured the traditional classics and,

Two members of the London Contemporary Dance Theatre, Anthony van Laast and Linda Gibbs in *The Calm* by one of LCDT's own choreographers, Siobhan Davies.

as we have said, revivals from the early years of this century. At popular prices, and with a popular repertory, the company reaches enormous audiences, both in Britain and abroad. As Dame Alicia Markova, one of its founders, has said: 'You must got out and dance and win a public; that it what matters.'

One of the most influential companies in trying to find a new audience and a new sort of ballet to offer them, was the Western Theatre Ballet, founded as a regional company by Elizabeth West and Peter Darrell in Bristol in 1957. Darrell gave the company a repertory whose aims are summed up in one of his first works for the WTB, *The Prisoners*. This is a story of two convicts who escape and take refuge with the elder man's wife. She falls in love with the younger convict, makes him murder her husband, and he finds himself at the end of the ballet imprisoned in her house by his sense of guilt. *The Prisoners* is very theatrical, and demonstrates how the WTB was looking for a more contemporary image for ballet that would relate it as much to the theatre as to dancing. Elizabeth West died tragically in a mountain accident in 1962 and Peter Darrell then became sole director of the company. He involved dramatists and producers in the creation of new works and the company's efforts to become a truly regional ballet were recognized in 1969 when it transferred to Glasgow to become, with Government support, the Scottish Ballet of today. The repertory now contains classics cleverly adapted for a small company – their *Giselle* is a very interesting new look at an old ballet and has been described as 'The Lovers of Nuremburg' – and new full-length ballets by Darrell like *The Tales of Hoffman*, a balletic version of the opera, and *Beauty and the Beast*, a modern re-working of the fairy tale. The company also produces a considerable number of short works by Darrell and other contemporary choreographers but its repertory, too, includes a beautiful staging of Bournonville's *La Sylphide*, his *La Ventana*, and dances from *William Tell*.

American ballets

While ballet was developing in Britain in the 1930s it was also taking root in America. There are ballet companies all over the United States but pride of place must go to the New York City Ballet. It is directed by Lincoln Kirstein, who has given George Balanchine total freedom to create. The result is a magnificent repertory in which the full genius of a master choreographer can be enjoyed. Balanchine is generous in allowing other companies to perform his works, but it is by the City Ballet that one sees them best danced. The greater part of Balanchine's choreography has a most austere appearance; dancers are simply clad and stage decoration is kept to a minimum. Balanchine is primarily interested in the relationship of dance and music. He has been more adventurous in the use of music (from the prettiest nineteenth-century tunes to the starkest of twentieth-century scores), than any other creator and, at their best, his ballets become the perfect visual expression of their score. In a piece like *Agon* the Stravinsky music lives before one's eyes – Balanchine helps an audience to understand music which otherwise they might not enjoy or appreciate. In *Agon*, as in so many of his ballets, the movement is absolutely right for the score. The contest – which is what the Greek title means – is portrayed by the dancers with not a little humour, but it is not necessary to look for meaning, since the virtuosity of the dancing is exciting and the shapes made by the dancers' bodies are beautiful.

Although *Agon* epitomizes the stripped-to-the-bone image that most people associate with Balanchine's work, it must not be forgotten than he can produce spectacular narrative pieces like *A Midsummer Night's Dream* and the perennial *Nutcracker*, as well as work as dramatic as *Night Shadow* (to be seen in the Festival Ballet's repertory) or as jolly as *Stars and Stripes*, an uproarious setting of Sousa marches which turns the classical girls of the company into drum majorettes.

One of Balanchine's most popular works is *Serenade*, almost the first ballet that he made in America. Because he was working with students from the newly opened School of American Ballet, Balanchine had to choreograph with whatever dancers were available at rehearsal. On the first day seventeen girls were present so he composed the opening scene for seventeen dancers; the next day there were only nine girls; the third day merely six. Nothing daunted, Balanchine choreographed with the numbers available and when male dancers started attending class they, too, were given roles. Incidents in rehearsal were introduced into the choreography, such as the time a girl fell and started to cry or another girl arrived late. Despite this method of work, *Serenade* is a ballet which says a great deal about the discipline and grace of classic movement and about what Balanchine believed was right for America. That he was correct in his belief is shown by the extraordinary flowering of classic dance in America under his guidance, and the enduring popularity of *Serenade* (with its lyrical Tchaikovsky score) in the repertories of many companies today.

A scene from Balanchine's *Serenade* danced by the New York City Ballet. The dancer in the centre is in the position which Balanchine incorporated into the ballet after a dancer had fallen during the rehearsals for the first performance.

The other major classical company in America, American Ballet Theatre, was begun as a brave enterprise in 1939, when Richard Pleasant and Lucia Chase decided to found a large cosmopolitan troupe to include many important figures in ballet at the time. Mikhail Fokine and the English choreographers, Antony Tudor and Andrée Howard were among the exceptionally large number of creators who were asked to stage ballets for the early seasons. By the mid 1940s the company had achieved remarkable artistic as well as popular success. Antony Tudor had staged *Pillar of Fire, Undertow* and *Romeo and Juliet* to music by Delius. These ballets showed the development of Tudor's concern for human relationships which he first explored in *Jardin aux Lilas*.

In the mid 1940s an American choreographer emerged with a bang. Jerome Robbins made *Fancy Free* for the Ballet Theatre in 1944. It is study of three sailors on shore leave pursuing two girls. The setting, a bar on a hot night in New York, the score, specially written by Leonard Bernstein, and the choreography, which translated dance hall styles of the period into balletic form, all added up to a smash hit. This was America dancing; the audience could see in the characters' behaviour as well as in their everyday clothes, that the dancers on the stage were people just like themselves.

Another American choreographer, Agnes de Mille, made a name for herself in following the fashion for ballets on American subjects. This trend had been started by Lincoln Kirstein who was concerned to stage American subjects, such as the outlaw *Billy the Kid*, and other works which dealt with everyday life in America, like *Filling Station* and *The Great American Goof*. Agnes de Mille had a great success with, among others, her cowboy ballet, *Rodeo*, for the Ballet Russe de Monte Carlo in 1942, and with her dances for the musical, *Oklahoma!*

Jerome Robbins was also concerned to show contemporary America on stage. He did not stay long with the Ballet Theatre, and was eventually to become most celebrated for his stagings on Broadway, culminating in *West Side Story*. For some time he had a company of his own, Ballets: USA, but ultimately he returned to the New York City Ballet and became one of its guiding spirits.

He produced, or revived, many works for the NYCB including his own version of *Afternoon of a Faun* which, unlike Nijinsky's Grecian setting, transplanted the story into a dance studio in New York one summer's day. Perhaps his greatest success in his recent NYCB period has been the hour long *Dances at a Gathering*, in which ten dancers are involved with Chopin piano music in a series of meetings, dances, and jokes that have delighted audiences wherever they are performed. With the loss of Robbins, the Ballet Theatre was never again to know a resident choreographer of his stature. In the twenty years since Robbins' departure, the Ballet Theatre has acquired works that range from the great classics to unspeakable modern novelties. What has sustained the company has often been the quality of its stars, usually foreign virtuoso dancers, whose popularity ensures an audience. The Danish Erik Bruhn, and the two defecting Kirov stars, Natalia Makarova and Mikhail Baryshnikov, have been three of the finest.

In 1959 Jerome Robbins formed his own ensemble, Ballets:USA, which existed intermittently for a period of three years to tour throughout the world. During its European performances, works like *New York Export Opus Jazz*, seen here, made a tremendous impact with the vitality and exuberance of the dancing.

The Ballet Theatre had always made use of the star system, even from its earliest years. In contrast, the NYCB has never wanted this sort of personality cult, and it is the excellence of the ensemble and even greater excellence of Balanchine's choreography that have earned the company its high reputation and ensured its progress every year. Of course the public will always have its favourites, and some of NYCB's dancers, like Edward Villella, have a popular following as great as any in America.

After the NYCB moved to Lincoln Center, the stage at the City Center was offered to a young company – the Joffrey Ballet – which had had popular success with a series of works that very cleverly captured public taste of the time. Most were short lived, but Robert Joffrey, the director of the company, has also staged revivals of ballets from the international repertory, as diverse as Massine's *Parade* and Frederick Ashton's *The Dream*.

In Russia

At the beginning of this century Diaghilev made the words 'Russian Ballet' the most glamorous and exciting in the theatre. This magic is still potent, and the first visit of the Bolshoy Ballet from Moscow to the West – a season at the Royal Opera House, Covent Garden in 1956 – made almost as big an impact as did the first Diaghilev season in the West. There was the grandeur and exuberant style that people had heard about, and there, too, was the legendary Galina Ulanova. With ballets like *Romeo and Juliet*, *The Fountain of Bakchisaray*, *Giselle* and the inevitable *Swan Lake*, the Bolshoy Ballet conquered the West, exciting audiences by the quality of the productions at that time, and by the power of the dancing.

That first season showed the cream of Soviet Ballet achievement since the Revolution: the magnificent training, based on the work of A Y Vaganova; the massive, careful and theatrically stunning productions (in *The Fountain of Bakchisaray* a house went up in flames); and the intensity of the dancers' performances.

For the stimulus of this first season the West must always be grateful. Thereafter it was possible to see in later visits by the Bolshoy, and by the peerless and aristocratic Kirov company from Leningrad, how superb the Russian dance training was, but how laboured and sterile was much of the choreography. This was because of the constant concern with political and national motives in the ballets' stories; everything seemed to have to have a message and a happy or uplifting ending. Typical of this is Yuri Grigorovitch's *Spartacus*. The story of the revolt by the Roman slaves is told with relentless energy but a good deal of monotony. Like so many Soviet ballets it is made bearable by the magnificence of the dancing and the dancers' total immersion in their roles. Despite the limited choreography and the soupy score, it is impossible not to be carried away by performances such as those given by Vasiliev as the doomed slave hero Spartacus, by Maximova as his beloved, and by Maris Liepa as the villainous Roman general Crassus.

Our picture of Russian ballet is of course incomplete. We know and love the superlative quality of the Leningrad dancers, for example, but we know little or nothing about the new ballets that are constantly staged in the Soviet Union – long works that deal with the political and social subjects that are thought so important by the authorities in Russia. We know even less about the activity in many of the big ballet companies that work in major cities throughout the Soviet Union – there are more than thirty-five of them. All have their own schools and occasionally an exceptionally gifted dancer will emerge from one.

Galina Ulanova as Juliet with Yuri Zhdanov as Romeo in the film of the Bolshoy Ballet's *Romeo and Juliet*. Ulanova was the most celebrated of Soviet ballerinas and several of her performances have been preserved on film.

The Bolshoy Ballet's Hollywood-spectacular treatment of *Spartacus*. Here Vladimir Vasiliev and his wife Ekaterina Maximova are shown in the final tableau.

In Europe

Denmark is a country with a ballet tradition nearly as old as that of Russia. The Royal Danish Ballet was made famous by August Bournonville in the nineteenth century; after his death there was no one who successfully continued making new ballets and the chief concern seemed to be the preservation of the Bournonville repertory and his system of training. Distinguished choreographers have sometimes worked briefly in Denmark, among them Fokine and Balanchine. It was not until 1954 that the Royal Danish Ballet plucked up courage to perform outside Denmark, when it presented a summer season in London. The enthusiasm of the British audiences for Bournonville's beautiful ballets and for the charm of the Danish style persuaded the Danes that they had something to offer the world of ballet, and since then the company has toured extensively with great success.

Travelling has also markedly changed the style of the company as the dancers have had Russian training as well as Bournonville classes. It is nevertheless because of the elegance and bounding grace of their style that the male dancers are sought after by companies throughout the world – and these qualities are the direct legacy from Bournonville.

The work of Harald Lander (1905–71) was primarily responsible for bringing the Danish Ballet to the attention of the world. When Fleming Flindt took over the company in 1965, after a brilliant career as a guest artist with several French and English companies, he determined to make the Royal Danish Ballet repertory more contemporary. In such ballets as *The Lesson, The Triumph of Death*, and *The Young Man Must Marry* (all based upon dramatic themes by the French playwright Eugène Ionesco) Flindt has captured a new audience. Young people, to whom the Bournonville ballets seem old-fashioned, have packed the New Stage in Copenhagen, especially for *The Triumph of Death*.

The Lesson is about an insane dance teacher who makes his pupil perform various mad steps he devises and finally murders her. The ballet is given a

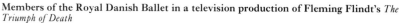

Members of the Royal Danish Ballet in a television production of Fleming Flindt's *The Triumph of Death*

'horror film' quality by the fact that we realize that this murder is going to be repeated over and over again. *The Triumph of Death*, to a pop score, is not so much a ballet as a terrific piece of theatre in which we are shown many aspects of Death and the collapse of civilization.

Young audiences have also found in Maurice Béjart and the Ballet du XXme Siècle from Brussels a company that offers them exactly the sort of ballet they want to see. The choreography may not be subtle or particularly inventive, but the theatrical impact is tremendous; the dancers are clearly absolutely dedicated, and Béjart's muddled message, which can involve Hindu mysticism and Rock, undeniably appeals to young people who are no longer interested in going to Opera Houses. Béjart plays to vast audiences each night in tents, halls and sports

Maurice Béjart's Ballet of the XXth Century appearing in the Boboli Gardens, Florence, in a spectacular especially commissioned for this setting.

Nederlands Dans Theatre in *Journal* with choreography by Louis Falco. This gimmicky ballet, with its armchairs and buckets of steaming dry ice and conversation from the cast, is typical of the willingness of NDT to experiment.

Alexandra Radius and Hans Ebbelaar in *Twilight* staged by the Dutch National Ballet.

stadia. Evening-long spectacles such as *Nijinsky, Clown of God* and *Golestan*, and Béjart's dreadful manglings of such great music as Beethoven's Ninth Symphony and *The Firebird* are immensely popular wherever he plays. The critics may despair but the box office beams.

It was in Belgium's neighbour Holland that a far more interesting kind of choreography developed after the 1939–45 war. There had been little or no tradition of Dutch classic ballet until a generation of young Dutch dancers and choreographers broke away from the staid Dutch National Ballet. These young men were to be associated with a new company, the Nederlands Dans Theater, which was started in 1959 and aimed at a far more modern presentation of dance. The company soon became celebrated not only for the vitality of its creations but also for the sheer number put on – the average was ten ballets every year. Men like Hans van Manen, Jaap Flier and the American choreographer Glen Tetley were responsible for making the company one of the most vital troupes in Europe. In many ways the NDT showed how a combination of classic ballet and modern dance could become a possibility. The repertory ranged from classical pieces like *Grand Pas Espagnol,* by another American, Benjamin Harkarvy, to

works which were based entirely on technique inspired by Martha Graham and other American teachers. Glen Tetley's *Mutations*, which he created with Hans van Manen, gained considerable notoriety because in certain sections the dancers appear nude.

The importance of the NDT has been its adventurous spirit and its willingness to try and find new ways in which dance could touch an audience. Its example has been felt in England (the Ballet Rambert owes it a great deal), and more importantly it influenced the Dutch National Ballet. This used to be a rather conventional company, with a repertory overloaded with revivals from the past, but it was revitalized in the 1970s and brought in Hans van Manen from the NDT to help its own choreographers, Rudi van Dantzig and Toer van Schayk, to update the identity of the company. In addition to *Giselle* and *Petrushka*, the Dutch National Ballet now offers works like van Dantzig's *Painted Birds* and van Manen's *Twilight*, which is also in the repertory of Britain's Royal Ballet.

Twilight is a duet for a boy and a girl, set in a city street with a power station in the background, which was painted by Jean Paul Vroom. As the sun sets, a pianist on stage performs a score by the American composer John Cage which makes use of a prepared piano – that is, an instrument in which various pieces of wood and metal have been inserted into the strings to produce eccentric sounds. The dance between the boy and the girl is very modern in its aggression, and the feeling of something like a duel between them is heightened by the fact that the girl wears vicious spiky-heeled shoes which she eventually takes off before flinging herself at the boy towards the ballet's end.

When Serge Lifar (last male star of the Ballet Russe) went to the Paris Opéra after the death of Diaghilev, he became responsible for the reawakening of ballet in France. As choreographer and principal dancer, Lifar made ballet fashionable with the Paris audience, and he also made reforms within the teaching system in the Paris Opéra School. For nearly thirty years Lifar led and inspired the Opéra. His choice of ballerinas, from Olga Spessivtseva, supreme classical product of the Maryinsky School in this century, to Yvette Chauviré, the greatest French ballerina since the Romantic era, and the Franco-Russian Nina Vyroubova, was an example to succeeding generations of young dancers.

The upheavals of the war and the German occupation of France resulted in an almost inevitable explosion of creative activity at the war's end. A group of young dancers eventually formed a small ballet company, Les Ballets des Champs Elysées, led by Roland Petit, who was trained at the Paris Opéra and guided by Diaghilev's former associates Boris Kochno and Jean Cocteau. The young company had talent and enthusiasm, and was responsible for some of the most beautiful designs any ballet company has known. For a brief period after the war the company delighted Europe with such ballets as *Les Forains*, a sad little incident about strolling players, and *Le Jeune Homme et la Mort*, which featured a superlative classic and dramatic artist, Jean Babilée, as a young man waiting in his garret for his girl friend. When she eventually arrives she is revealed to be not a girl but Death itself. The impact – especially in London – was tremendous, but the company was short-lived, and Roland Petit and his wife Renée Jeanmaire soon left to form their own troupe. Their Ballet de Paris exploited Jeanmaire's very considerable glamour – most spectacularly in a version of *Carmen* in which the now celebrated 'Zizi' Jeanmaire acquired world fame – but it no longer had the artistic guidance that had made the Ballets des Champs Elysées so exciting, and soon both Petit and Jeanmaire moved into the world of spectacular stage shows, films and cabaret.

The Paris Opéra meantime continued under Lifar's guidance until the late 1950s. Thereafter a series of caretaker directors seemed unable to do anything to stem the gradual decline in creativity and interest. In recent years a serious attempt has been made to bring in modern dance, and in 1973 the stately Opéra invited the ultra modern Merce Cunningham from New York to stage an austere, full evening ballet: *Un Jour ou Deux*.

Jean Babilée rehearsing for the role of the Joker in *Jeu de Cartes* by Janine Charrat. He was gifted with extraordinary virtuosity and phenomenal dramatic power.

A livelier view of ballet exists in the Ballet Théâtre Contemporain, a company founded in 1968 which is resident in the French provinces. Dedicated to new choreography and good designing, the BTC is more representative of the new generation of French dance than any other companies that exist in Paris or the provinces. The lightweight *Hopop*, with its pop dancing and pop design, shows how open minded the BTC is. It is a company that welcomes every new development in painting, in music and in choreography. For this reason it represents a serious attempt to further the cause of ballet by bringing it to a wider audience.

As in Holland, ballet in Germany is a post-war development. For the first half of this century dance in Germany was the gloomiest kind of modern dance, very soul-searching and earthbound. A few brave spirits kept the flag of classicism faintly flying, but it was the example of the Stuttgart company which provided the boost for ballet in Germany. In 1960 John Cranko took over the company in Stuttgart. With his ballerina Marcia Haydee, and leading dancers Richard Cragun and Egon Madsen, he aroused tremendous enthusiasm for ballet in an ever-growing German audience. At the time of his death in 1973 Cranko's company was one of the most interesting in Europe. It had achieved world fame and had encouraged other German cities to give greater attention to classical ballet.

The future of ballet in Germany, as everywhere, depends on the emergence of new choreographers. Throughout Europe, despite vast state subsidies for ballet in some cities, there is a chronic shortage of good choreography and good ballets today. In Vienna and Milan, for example, ballet is still forced to take second place to the opera, and the majority of productions are re-stagings of the classics, graced by guest stars. The public in both these cities is notoriously unenterprising in its taste, and reluctant to recognize what is going on in the ballet world elsewhere.

above left **Dancers of the Ballet-Théâtre Contemporain in** *Hopop*. This jolly ballet has designs by César, and the dancers' tights are decorated with scenes and characters from strip cartoons.

below left **Richard Cragun and Marcia Haydee of the Stuttgart Ballet in John Cranko's** *The Taming of the Shrew*. The battles between the dashing virtuoso Cragun as Petruchio and the classically exquisite Haydee as Kate the Shrew run the full range of comedy, from broad farce to delicate wit.

PAYING FOR
THE BALLET

The idea that ballet has always been financially viable, let alone profitable, is utterly and totally wrong: paying for ballet is still the daily nightmare of every company, and every organisation that has to provide funds for dance. From its beginning and until the end of the nineteenth century, ballet was almost always paid for by the monarchs and princes whose servants the dancers were. In Imperial Russia the Tsar was willing to make good any additional financial deficit from his privy purse; with few exceptions the other state ballet companies were financed by their respective governments – and when Noverre went to Stuttgart in 1760 one of the attractions of the company was the prodigality of the Grand Duke of Wurttemberg who was happy to dip deep into his treasury to pay for the theatre he loved. A few private theatrical managers during the Romantic era – Dr Véron at the Paris Opéra and Benjamin Lumley in London – made money by astute publicity and by cashing in on the vast popularity of the ballerinas of the day. But in our century we can see just how ballet's financial troubles have developed. Diaghilev was the first to highlight this fact. His company was notorious for its financial problems – his very first season in Paris, just one month's performances, produced a deficit of £5,000, a large sum for 1909 – and part of Diaghilev's genius lay in his ability to charm funds from wealthy friends and patrons. The twenty years of the Ballet Russe was scarred by recurrent money problems. It was constantly rescued by gifts from friends and admirers – among them Coco Chanel, the *couturière*, and Lord Rothermere the newspaper magnate. Other companies of the 1920s – the Ida Rubenstein Ballet, Rolf de Maré's Ballet Suédois – were sustained by private fortunes, as was the Grand Ballet du Marquis de Cuevas during the 1940s and 1950s, and latterly the Harkness Ballet. A very few companies somehow managed to make ends meet through astute management, in particular the pre-war Ballets Russes of Colonel de Basil, and the London Festival Ballet in the years before it received support from government and local council sources.

In Britain there was no tradition of royal patronage of the theatre at all and British ballet was first financed on the merest of shoestrings. That great woman Lilian Baylis (1874–1937) was the true founder both of our national opera and ballet and our National Theatre. These all sprang from her endeavours at the Old Vic Theatre during the 1920s and 1930s. She produced Shakespeare and opera in English, and provided a home for Ninette de Valois' plans for an English national ballet company. By skilful budgeting and incessant appeals for funds she helped each of her enterprises to flourish. Stories about 'the Lady' (as Miss Baylis was known) and her constant appeals for money are legion. On one occasion, when invited to speak at a City luncheon, she began with the words: 'Ladies and gentlemen: if any of you are about to die . . . please remember the Old Vic in your Will.'

The war years were to make state patronage absolutely essential. CEMA (the Council for the Encouragement of Music and the Arts) was brought into being to start paying for the arts in response to the enormously increased public demand for entertainment of every kind during the war. When the war ended and the Royal Opera House, Covent Garden was reopened as a permanent home for ballet and opera, there came the need for consistent and continuous support. By that time CEMA had been transformed into what is now the Arts Council of Great Britain which is responsible for providing funds for all the arts on a national basis – orchestras, art galleries, museums, regional theatres as well as ballet, opera and the national theatre companies in London.

Today the Arts Council takes direct financial responsibility for every one of the ballet companies operating in Britain. The tragedy is that funds are never adequate. By 1974 the Royal Opera House was receiving a grant – for both opera and ballet – of £2,550,000 per annum. But inflation and the appalling costs of everything from ballet shoes to electricity means that this sum is barely enough to cover operating costs, let alone encompass the constant need for new productions. The Arts Council grant is related to the box office receipts; it matches and exceeds the actual box office takings.

Although the sum at the disposal of the opera and ballet may seem enormous, it is worth recording that it is nowhere near as great as the funds that are made available for the ballet and opera companies in cities like Hamburg and Vienna.

How is this money spent? For a proper breakdown of payments you should refer to the annual reports published by the Royal Opera House, which show the cost of productions, of salaries, and all the overheads. In 1973 a lavish staging of *The Sleeping Beauty* cost £55,627; one act ballets can vary in cost from the £9,387 for *Laborintus* by Glen Tetley, to the £1,083 for Hans van Manen's *Grosse Fugue*; the Opera House orchestra alone cost £414,000; salaries paid to the dancers were £486,000; while the New Group's touring expenses amounted to £314,000. The Royal Ballet gets through more than 15,000 pairs of pointe shoes in a year.

The splendours and miseries of touring. Members of the Festival Ballet feeding the pigeons in St Mark's Square, Venice show one side of the story. Some of The Royal Ballet touring group trudging uphill from Leeds station in search of lodgings shows the other.

The general reader, of course, is entitled to ask why it is that a successful musical, employing a big cast and an orchestra, can make money while no opera or ballet company can do anything but struggle to stay within its budget. The answer lies partly in the very considerable number of people involved in keeping an opera house open and maintaining the general running and administration of the companies. It also lies in the larger number of artists involved, in the continually changing and developing repertory, in constant rehearsals, and in the responsibility of the companies to offer the greatest artists and the highest standards on every occasion. The Royal Ballet and the Royal Opera represent two peaks of the arts in Britain. They are vital in representing an image of the nation that is recognized and admired throughout the world, which also encourages foreign visitors to come and see them in their home theatre.

For The Royal Ballet too there are the additional expenses of touring through the regions and abroad. These expenses are quite out of proportion to the box office receipts. Seat prices outside London cannot be put as high as those in the metropolis. The very fact of touring means an immediate increase in costs – in transportation of dancers, musicians, and sets and costumes, and in accommodation (a 'touring' allowance of between £20–£30 a week for every member of the corps de ballet alone was being paid in 1974). Further foreign

travel is now becoming prohibitive for the large company, and major tours
abroad are dependent upon the generosity of private organizations who donate
grants to bolster state aid. Without these, much touring would be impossible.
(Such considerations affect every company with the exception of Soviet troupes;
the Russian Government, recognizing their importance as cultural institutions
and ambassadors, subsidizes them up to the hilt.)

The pattern is the same for each of the ballet companies working in Britain.
Although grants may seem generous, the cost of ballet far exceeds any other
branch of the theatre except opera; the need to tour both a company and its
orchestra and scenery, the continual wear and tear on productions, the need for
rehearsal time, all mean a constant concern for economy which is a continuous
headache for the administrators and directors of ballet companies.

Although we may complain about the inadequacy of government funds,
European companies are the envy of American troupes. In the United States
there is no specific government aid for the theatre. Ballet companies depend
financially upon the generosity of the great foundations, like the Ford
Foundation, for grants which are sometimes matched by complementary
funding from state or civic authorities. In 1966 the Ford Foundation made
$7,000,000 available to the New York City Ballet and in 1974 it gave $3,100,000,

which was matched by the City of New York. The American Ballet Theatre in 1973 received a similar grant. But both companies constantly have to hold out their begging bowls in the form of fund raising galas. In America, unlike England, there are still people who will pay vast sums for tickets, and it is possible to raise the kind of money which could never be made from even the most expensive gala at the Royal Opera House. Moreover, American tax laws encourage such generosity through tax deductible allowances. But the nagging worry is always there; there is no guarantee of how much money will come in, and planning for the future, made possible in England by the certainty of government support, is always precarious in the United States.

The smaller dance companies, particularly those working in the modern dance medium, are forced to rely either on private generosity – Martha Graham's work was made possible by very generous private donations – or on small grants from various foundations. This financial insecurity brings even greater artistic insecurity. Companies can only work for part of the year; dancers leave to find well paid work in the commercial theatre or in the cinema; many of the greatest choreographers have to teach to earn a living; some of the most revered names in modern dance use whatever money they themselves may earn to keep their companies in existence. It says much for their dedication that they are prepared to face the most grinding touring schedules and teaching assignments to enable them to continue their work. Whatever the rewards, they do not include money.

The 1970s have been marked by appalling problems of inflation in every aspect of public and private life and the theatre, no less than the housewife, has fallen victim to rising costs and bills that seem to double themselves overnight. A production which might have cost £20,000 or $50,000 ten years ago, will now cost £70,000 or $175,000. From shoes to the rates of pay for stage hands and orchestral musicians, from the cost of materials for costumes to the cost of telephone calls in the opera house, from the building costs of sets to the running of the canteen, prices have spiralled with alarming rapidity.

The result is being felt, and will be felt for years, in the necessity to cut back, to scrimp and save. In London, for example, Sadler's Wells Theatre, now an 'hotel' theatre for many visiting dance companies, is faced with the prospect of closure unless government subvention is increased. The Royal Opera House can state without fear of contradiction that unless government support is increased at least to keep up with inflation, the same fate may await even that theatre.

Without wishing to seem too depressing, it is important that the public realize just how serious is the present financial situation for ballet, opera and the theatre. As this book was being written, one American company had to close and now two more face extinction. In London, the plight of Sadler's Wells Theatre and the financial problems of the Royal Opera House have yet to be properly alleviated. A lunatic situation has been reached where it is less expensive to keep a company in rehearsal than to put it on a stage.

BALLET ON FILM AND TELEVISION

It is impossible to overestimate the importance of the cinema in the twentieth century. History has been preserved, and most of the great men and women of the past seventy years can be seen as they were in life. Alas, this is not true of dancers. Although by the time that the Diaghilev Ballet came to the West cinema techniques were quite advanced, there is no film at all of the Diaghilev Ballet in performance, nothing of Karsavina or Nijinsky and only some short clips of Anna Pavlova, and the best of these accidental – Pavlova was a friend of Douglas Fairbanks and one day in Hollywood he decided to film her rehearsing. Thus a few of her dances can be seen, notably *Christmas* and *The Californian Poppy* and, oddly, part of *The Dying Swan*. Towards the end of this little solo she suddenly giggles and stops, and then redoes a brief section of it. But we do not even have a complete record of this single most famous solo of the century. It seems little short of criminal negligence that so little attempt was made to preserve something of the greatness of dancing at a time when ballet was blessed with such superb performers.

It is thanks to amateur photographers that records survive of a few important artists. Probably the most celebrated is a short film in the possession of Dame Marie Rambert which shows Olga Spessivtseva in two minutes of *Giselle* . . . those two minutes tell us more about her peerless art than any number of books and photographs. A few tiny snippets of film exist of artists of the 1900s, and there are some examples on celluloid of the work of major dancers from the 1930s onwards, nearly all in private collections.

Because ballet was thought to be a very rarified entertainment at this time, film companies were reluctant to take any chances of losing money, and there were no organizations concerned with the actual preservation of the art of ballet on film. Conversely, there is some good dancing preserved in the films of the

Anna Pavlova with Laurent Novikov in *Christmas*.

1930s, and the spectacular Hollywood movies of the period can show just how extravagantly America was able to indulge its audiences. Films and dance scenes directed by Busby Berkeley are still magnificent fun, and Fred Astaire and Ginger Rogers and Jessie Matthews were among the most popular stars of the period. But these artists worked in the cinema and were presented in cinematic terms – their dances were specifically designed to fit in to the film and be part of its action. They also made use of possibilities of the camera for tricks of every kind.

The fantastic development of the American musical in the early 1940s resulted not only in a much greater use of dancing and actual ballets in the musicals, but their eventual transfer to the screen. *Oklahoma!*, *On the Town*, *Call me Madam* and above all Jerome Robbins' *West Side Story* are good examples. The taste for brilliant dance in the setting of a musical film can also be seen in *Seven Brides for Seven Brothers*, in which Michael Kidd, a former dancer with American Ballet Theatre, used some of the best dancers from that company.

There have also been various attempts to present ballet itself in the cinema. In the early 1940s Hollywood made versions of two ballets by Leonide Massine, *Gaieté Parisienne* and *Spanish Rhapsody*, neither of which gives much idea of how the ballets looked on stage although they do contain glimpses of the star dancers of the time. Other experiments were made at filming ballet, and Walt Disney even included an odd ballet sequence in his *Fantasia*, but the most successful ballet film – in box office terms – came after the war when Michael Powell and Emeric Pressburger made *The Red Shoes*. Its story is nonsensical, and it was totally unlike the real world of ballet which it pretended to show. *The Red Shoes*

Fred Astaire and Eleanor Powell in MGM's *Broadway Melody of 1940.*

starred Moira Shearer, then a leading dancer with The Royal Ballet, and also made use of the talents of Leonide Massine and Robert Helpmann. It contained a ballet choreographed by Helpmann expressly for the cinema in which good use was made of the camera's tricks – at the end Helpmann himself turned into a newspaper. Although condemned by almost every film and ballet critic, *The Red Shoes* was nevertheless an enormous box office success not only in Britain but throughout America. It did something to contribute to the growing popularity of ballet, partly because Shearer, a dancer of remarkable prettiness, epitomized to the general public the image of a ballerina.

For many years our only knowledge of Soviet Ballet came from boringly made films which showed some of their greatest dancers. A priceless record survives of Galina Ulanova dancing the Act II pas de deux from *Swan Lake* with Konstantin Sergeyev, although they seem to be dancing it on a piece of old carpet. Similarly, there is a dazzling display of virtuosity by Natalia Dudinskaya and Vakhtang Chabukiany in part of *La Bayadère*, although in this case they seem to be dancing on a piece of looking glass. The films may be inadequate but the performances are superb. Unfortunately, this is too often the judgement that has to be passed upon ballet films.

Nevertheless, there do exist a considerable number of fragments on film of dancers over the past thirty years: in every case the camera is really being used to provide an animated snapshot of the artists concerned. Rarely if ever are the possibilities of the cinema itself explored to enhance the dancer or the choreography. The reason is that the camera's lens is unable to encompass the depth and range of movement patterns (which are the essence of choreography) without giving the audience what is really just a bird's eye view. If the cameraman and director decide to zoom in to a close up shot, all continuity is lost and the camera immediately emphasizes one single part of the dancer's anatomy – it is idiotic to break up the great Act II pas de deux in *Swan Lake* to show Odette's head or some detail of her foot. There have been attempts – all too rare – at making choreography for the cinema, in which the camera becomes a participant in the action so that it shows the audience exactly what the choreographer intends the audience to see. The best examples of this are the ballet sequence in *The Red Shoes* and, of course, *West Side Story* and the works of Busby Berkeley in the 1930s. A recent example in which choreographer and camera were happily united was *The Tales of Beatrix Potter*. Sir Frederick Ashton's dances were specifically designed for cinema, not stage, and by the use of perspective and mammoth properties, the dancers could be turned into tiny mice or squirrels and Michael Coleman in the character of Jeremy Fisher was seen floating on the leaf of a water lily before embarking on a brilliant solo. Some of the finest dancers of The Royal Ballet were involved and Ashton himself appeared as Mrs Tiggywinkle.

Happily there have also been serious attempts to preserve great ballets and great dancers on film. A charming and evocative short film, *Le Spectre de la Danse*, was made of the great French ballerina Nina Vyroubova, and when the

Alexander Grant as Peter Rabbit in *The Tales of Beatrix Potter*, **a ballet choreographed for the cinema by Sir Frederick Ashton.**

Bolshoy first came to London in 1956 Paul Czinner devised a system which enabled him to preserve Galina Ulanova's Giselle with maximum speed. After a performance one night a series of eleven cine-cameras were installed in various parts of the auditorium of the Royal Opera House and the entire production was performed again for the cameras. The result was eleven different views of the ballet, which were then cut and edited to present a valid record of that *Giselle*. Paul

Czinner later made two films of The Royal Ballet using the same system, and in them are preserved worthy records, especially of Margot Fonteyn as the Firebird and as Odette and Ondine. Later Paul Czinner also filmed MacMillan's *Romeo and Juliet* with Fonteyn and Nureyev, but the dancers came to the film studio to perform, so it can hardly be counted a successful record of the ballet as it was seen on the stage.

Two recent films have benefited from Rudolf Nureyev's enormous popularity; he can be seen in *I am a Dancer* and also in the Australian Ballet's full length *Don Quixote* which he also helped direct.

In Russia the decision was made early to preserve ballets and performances, most successfully with Ulanova in Lavrovsky's *Romeo and Juliet*, rather less so with productions of *The Sleeping Beauty* and *Swan Lake* in which most of the choreography was lost in 'clever' camera angles. The Russians have shown more enterprise in filming ballet than the West but most of the resultant works seem indifferent to Western eyes.

For anyone really interested in catching up with ballet round the world, there are sometimes opportunities to see rarities of the dance scene, for example the Chinese have filmed a couple of their most popular ballets, heavy with political messages.

Television

From the very earliest days of television there was a concern to show dancing in its many forms. An early experiment in the late 1930s was a story written by Antony Tudor for Maude Lloyd and the television cameras. The Vic Wells Ballet was televised in 1937 in *Les Patineurs*. Since the war ballet has featured a great deal on television. There have been educational programmes as well as star spots for ballet in variety shows and gala performances. Generally, viewers are shown pas de deux taken out of context, performed by famous dancers of the day. But the most important contribution to television ballet has been the work of Margaret Dale, for many years a principal dancer with the Royal Ballet who became a television producer and director for the BBC. She brings a unique qualification to her task, in that she knows about dancing as a performer. Her transfers of repertory works to the small screen are important because she is able to adjust the productions and the choreography to the conditions of the medium. Her presentations of *Giselle*, *La Fille mal Gardée* and *Coppélia* (all in black and white), for example, gave a true picture of the ballets. They remain models of what such television ballets should be.

By contrast, some of the spectacular colour productions of The Royal Ballet which have been televised from the stage of the Royal Opera House have suffered because there has been no attempt to give anything but a bird's eye view of the ballet as the camera can pick it up.

Careful scrutiny of the weekly television magazines will usually reveal at least one dance programme a month. Some television companies have made a real effort to cater for the dance public; the BBC has done a great deal, of course, and has also shown ballet programmes made by European and American television companies. Granada TV has recently invited very interesting guest companies (the American dancers Paul Taylor, Twyla Tharp and the Dance Theatre of Harlem) to appear as well as commissioning new works from British choreographers. Germany has done a great deal to record ballets for television showing and also to create special works. In 1973 the New York City Ballet was invited to Berlin for over a month so that television cameras could record performances of Balanchine ballets danced by Balanchine's own company and supervised by him. This is an example of the work that television can do both in preserving ballets and also in making them available to a much larger public than could ever get in – or afford to get in – to theatres.

Of course some of the programmes do ballet a great disservice, for instance

Dame Margot Fonteyn and Michael Somes, with members of The Royal Ballet, during a television production of the last act of *The Sleeping Beauty* in New York in 1955. It drew fantastic viewing figures.

In 1953 BBC Television filmed Fokine's *Les Sylphides* and assembled a distinguished Royal Ballet cast, and called upon several great authorities to assist in the production. From left to right, Lydia Sokolova (an Englishwoman who became a star of the Diaghilev ballet), Cyril Beaumont (the eminent historian), Svetlana Beriosova, Tamara Karsavina (who danced in the original production of 1909), Christian Simpson (the producer), Dame Alicia Markova, and Violetta Prokhorova Elvin (a Soviet dancer who married an Englishman and came to London where she became a principal of The Royal Ballet).

some emanating from the French television service have been appalling. Perfectly dreadful choreography and performances, in costumes of matching horror, can give ballet an awful name. Ballet lovers are offended, and the prejudices of people who know nothing about ballet are confirmed.

But for the balletgoer there can never be enough dancing on television. Sometimes because television companies lack courage (they live in fear of low ratings), and sometimes because of trouble with the dancers' and stagehands' unions (a problem which has recently prevented the BBC from showing any British ballet), opportunities have been missed. An incidental pleasure for the ballet lover are such television documentaries as BBC Television's portraits of Diaghilev, Pavlova, Dame Marie Rambert, Dame Ninette de Valois and Leonide Massine.

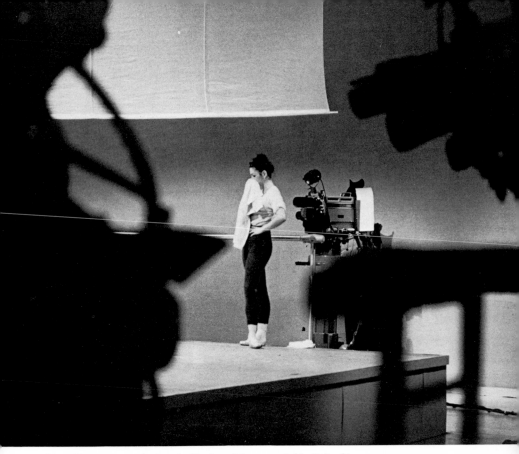

Lynn Seymour seen during the filming of the remarkable *Ballet Class* programme on BBC Television. It showed Peter Wright, associate director of The Royal Ballet, giving a class to a group of principals of the company.

A few years ago Thames Television made a notable contribution with *Ballet for All*. It was a series of programmes by Peter Brinson which was linked with The Royal Ballet's demonstration group of the same name, and gave a history and appreciation of ballet as a theatre art.

The enormous popularity and influence of television suggest that it has only just scratched the surface of what it might do for ballet as it has begun to do for the other arts. The success of Lord Clark's series *Civilisation* and Dr Jacob Bronowski's *The Rise of Man* is a tribute to the power of the medium to stimulate people's minds and awareness of the arts and sciences. And, of course, television is the most powerful method of 'selling' by advertisement. As the great ballet enthusiast Arnold Haskell observed 'Television sells detergents and chocolates, why not ballet?'

POSTSCRIPT

Ballet has never been more popular than it is today. The demand for good ballets and for great dancers has meant that all over the world greater attention is being paid to the establishment of national schools of ballet which will feed the growing number of companies. In Cuba, Canada and Australia there are now excellent schools, established within the last few decades. Every year new talent emerges.

Twenty years ago it would have been possible to write a chapter in a book of this kind about the most famous dancers of the era. Just to list the internationally celebrated names today would require the same chapter, even without mentioning their individual gifts. Throughout this book we have made passing reference to some of the great dancers who give so much pleasure to so many people and have so enriched ballet, but we feel that it is more fitting to pay tribute here to the corps de ballet of the major companies of the world.

You cannot judge the greatness of a company by its stars – the true evidence lies in the rank and file of the ensemble and, if we must single out any groups, we would like to offer our grateful thanks to the artists of The Royal Ballet's corps de ballet and those of the Leningrad State Kirov Ballet. They are living witness to the magnificence of their respective companies and to their schools. The greatest ballerinas – Margot Fonteyn, Galina Ulanova – could not have achieved their eminence without the setting provided by all those swans and wilis. If the ballerina represents the most obvious image of a company and a style, it is a style that is to be seen throughout the company. If Fonteyn and Ulanova represent the essence of English and Russian dancing, so too does the work of the corps de ballet that sustain them.

Any company can buy the services of star dancers and some managements have relied upon one or two starry names to get bookings and audiences for companies which, without them, would draw neither engagements nor public. But the making of a corps de ballet takes time, teaching of the finest quality, and a real sense of dedication. We began this book by talking about the importance of the school and we finish by acknowledging the vital contribution made by the corps de ballet and the teachers and répétiteurs who ensure that standards are not only maintained but constantly improved.

Much as we enjoy the dancing of those ballerinas and male dancers whose names are household words, we give our final thanks to the dancers, often unnamed in the programme, who are the mainstay of the art of ballet throughout the world.

GLOSSARY

The development of ballet technique has been a gradual process over nearly three hundred years. By the end of the seventeenth century the five positions had been codified and during the next three hundred years professional dancers, particularly the men, developed ever more elaborate steps. By the beginning of the nineteenth century there was a greater equality of skill between men and women, and most of the terms described in this glossary were already in use – although the way they were danced was very different from the way they are today. Quite a lot is known about technique in the early years of the nineteenth century, thanks to the instruction manuals of Carlo Blasis, and we are on even more familiar ground by the time we get to the Romantic movement and the first very tentative rising on to pointe. Not until late in the nineteenth century was the blocked pointe shoe a common feature of theatrical dancing. It is very important to remember that the way in which steps are performed, and the style of the dancers, changes all the time. Each age expects something different from its dancers and yesterday's feats of virtuosity are often commonplaces for the next generation.

Although modern dance began in direct opposition to classical ballet, there is now considerable exchange of ideas between the two systems. This glossary however is simply a guide to some of the more obvious terms connected with ballet. When you see a modern dance company the differences as well as the similarities with ballet will be easy to recognize.

Adagio   (French, adage) Slow movement stressing balance, also used as a term for the slow section of partnering in a pas de deux.

Allegro   All light and fast movements, as in music.

Arabesque   A pose in which the body is supported on one leg with the other leg extended behind, usually with one arm in front and the other behind, to give the longest possible line between finger tips and toes.

Attitude   A position inspired by the statue of Mercury by the Renaissance sculptor Gian Bologna (1524–1608). The dancer stands on one leg while the other is extended to the back at an angle of 90° with the knee bent. One arm is raised and the other extended to the side.

Balletomane   Someone addicted to ballet. The word was first used in Russia of men who attended every single performance sitting in the front of the stalls. Now it is used for devotees all over the world who can be found in every part of every theatre in which ballets are performed. Arnold Haskell introduced the word to the Western public with his best selling book *Balletomania* (1934).

Ballon The bounciness of a dancer. Different from elevation, ballon is really the elasticity with which a step is performed.

Barre A wooden pole fixed horizontally on the walls of a ballet studio at roughly waist height. The dancers use it during their first exercise to provide light support. Except for more strenuous limbering exercises, their fingers only rest on the barre.

Batterie (beats) The term applied to all movements in which the feet beat together or one foot beats against another. See entrechat.

Bourrée (Pas de bourrée.) Movement on full or half pointe by a sequence of very small, even steps which gives the impression that the dancer is gliding across the stage. Nadia Nerina says that pas de bourrée should look like a string of perfectly matched pearls.

Classical Ballet This terms refers both to the system of training and to a small number of ballets. The training is that of the academic style as perfected in the nineteenth and twentieth centuries. The ballets are those survivors from the nineteenth century which were in the main created or preserved in Russia – *Swan Lake, The Sleeping Beauty, The Nutcracker, Giselle, La Bayadère* etc.

Corps de ballet The rank and file of the company. Great corps de ballet are rarer than great ballerinas.

Divertissement The collection of dances that usually comprise the last act of jollifications in the big nineteenth century ballets. They were an opportunity to show off the principals and soloists of the company, and usually had nothing whatsoever to do with the rest of the ballet, e.g. the last acts of *The Sleeping Beauty* and *Raymonda*.

Elevation The ability to jump high in the air; the necessary refinement is the quietness of the landing.

Enchaînement Any combination of steps, in class or more usually on stage.

Entrechat A jump during which the dancer rises straight in the air and the feet change their position with regard to one another four, six, eight or, exceptionally, ten times.

Épaulement	The placing of the head and shoulders in relation to the rest of the body to give harmony and variety to a position.
Five positions	The basic positions of the feet with which most steps in classical ballet begin or end. They were known and in use by the end of the seventeenth century. They are excellently described and illustrated in G B L Wilson's *Dictionary of Ballet*.
Fouetté	The usual name for a step in which the dancer stands on one leg and uses the other in a whipping motion to help the turning of the body. Almost always performed by the female dancer on pointe, the most celebrated example of fouettés is in the coda of the Black Swan pas de deux where the ballerina is called upon to turn no fewer than thirty-two.
Jeté	A spring from one foot to the other. A jump finishing in any required position.
Mime	The use of facial and bodily expressions to convey narrative. There is a traditional language of gesture developed from the Italian theatre which was much used in nineteenth century ballets. It still survives and can still be effective in the presentation of some of the great classics.
Pas	Literally a step (French), it also can be used to mean a whole solo dance (pas seul) or a dance for any number of performers, e.g. pas de deux, pas de trois, pas de quatre etc.
Pas de deux	The duet for the male and female principals of the ballet which is considered the highlight of the choreography of a scene. In the nineteenth century ballets, a pas de deux had a strict construction: 1. the entrée (the entrance for the two dancers); 2. male variation; 3. female variation; 4. coda, the culminating display of virtuosity. Much of the quality in pas de deux depends upon the skilful partnership between the two dancers and upon the man's dignity and pride in presenting his ballerina to best advantage.
Pas d'action	Any scene in which the narrative of the ballet is carried forward in dancing.
Pirouette	A complete turn of the body performed on one leg. There are many kinds of pirouette; the difference between them depends upon the position of the body and the direction in which it turns. The vital matter for the dancer in multiple pirouettes is 'spotting'. The dancer fixes his eyes on one spot while the body turns; the head is the last and fastest part to turn and returns to the same spot thus avoiding giddiness.

Plié	A leg bend (French, plier = to bend) As an exercise it is performed at the beginning of every class. Pliés are done at the barre to start warming up the muscles. Pliés are also the spring from which all jumps start and the essential landing mechanism from a jump without which the foot would crash rigid to the ground and be injured.
Pointes	A dancer is on pointe when she stands on the tips of her toes. This development was gradually established in the first half of the nineteenth century. The female dancer's shoes were at that time soft slippers and it was not until the Italian shoemakers, later in the century, produced a stiffened, blocked toe shoe that dancing on pointes became general. In this century the quality of the blocked shoes and the development of the training has meant that dancing on pointe is a commonplace of ballet. Very rarely, in character roles, a male dancer will go on pointe.
Romantic Ballet	A term originally used to describe the period between 1830 and 1850 when ballet became tremendously popular in Western Europe thanks to the participation of ballerinas like Taglioni, Elssler and Grisi. It is now used to describe any ballet that is romantic in mood.
Tour en l'air	The dancer springs straight into the air and turns once, twice (double tours en l'air – a necessary technical feat for most male dancers), and very exceptionally thrice. A triple tour en l'air is, in fact, so fast that it is seldom noticed by lay members of the audience. (See Richard Cragun.)
Turn out	The turning out of the leg from the hip joints so that the foot may be seen to be held at an angle of 90°. It applies only to classical ballet. It gives the dancers freedom of movement and beauty of line.
Tutu	The usual term for the very short fluffy skirt worn by ballerinas in classical ballets, such as *Swan Lake*, etc. Made of many layers of tarlatan, the tutu has become the accepted dress for female dancers even in contemporary classical works.
Virtuosity	The supreme technical skill which marks out a principal dancer. Though never an end in itself, great technical ability is always exciting to watch and is often displayed in ostentatious pas de deux. Virtuosity should be the servant of artistry and true virtuosity is often unnoticed by an audience.

BRIEF BIOGRAPHIES

This selection of entries covers people and organizations to whom passing reference is made in the book. It does not pretend to be complete. For the best reference book see *A Dictionary of Ballet* by G B L Wilson, latest edition Adam and Charles Black 1974.

Ashton, Sir Frederick b. 1904 English dancer and choreographer whose ballets from 1930 onwards have been the mainstay of British ballet. Director of The Royal Ballet 1964–70, he shaped the identity of that company through a magnificent series of ballets.

Bakst, Léon 1866–1924 Russian painter whose designs for the Diaghilev Ballet revolutionized stage decor, particularly through their use of bright colours.

Balanchine, George b. 1904 Trained in the Russian Imperial Schools, he left Russia in 1925 and joined the Diaghilev Ballet as choreographer and dancer. In 1933 he went to the USA where, with the support of Lincoln Kirstein, he started a school and company, which grew into the New York City Ballet of today.

Baryshnikov, Mikhail b. 1948 A star of the Leningrad Kirov Ballet who defected in Canada in 1974, he is one of the outstanding classical dancers of today.

Béjart, Maurice b. 1927 French dancer and choreographer. Founder and Director of the enormously popular company The Ballet of the Twentieth Century.

Benois, Alexandre 1870–1960 Russian-born painter who was a great influence upon Diaghilev and who designed many of the Diaghilev company's early successes.

Blair, David 1932–1976 English dancer who became a principal of The Royal Ballet creating many roles, notably Colas in *La Fille mal Gardée*.

Blasis, Carlo 1797–1878 Italian dancer and teacher whose theories and writings were vital to the development of ballet training during the nineteenth century.

Bolm, Adolf 1884–1951 Russian dancer who joined the Diaghilev company in 1909 and caused a sensation in Paris with his virile dancing in *Prince Igor*. From 1918 he lived and worked in America.

Bournonville, August 1805–79 Founding father of the Royal Danish Ballet.

Bruce, Christopher b. 1945 Outstanding English dancer and choreographer whose career has been spent mostly with the Ballet Rambert.

Bruhn, Erik b. 1928 A Danish dancer renowned throughout the world as a classical dancer and an outstanding dance actor.

Chauviré, Yvette b. 1917 Great French ballerina particularly celebrated for her interpretation of *Giselle*.

Cohan, Robert b. 1925 American modern dancer who worked for many years with Martha Graham. Since 1967 he has been Artistic Director and choreographer for the London Contemporary Dance Theatre.

Coleman, Michael b. 1940 English dancer, a principal of The Royal Ballet, who excels both in virtuoso and dramatic roles.

Cragun, Richard b. 1944 American dancer who became principal dancer of the Stuttgart Ballet and created many roles for John Cranko. A fine actor and brilliant dancer – one of the few to perform triple tours en l'air.

Cranko, John 1927–1973 South African born dancer and choreographer who first made his name creating several ballets for The Royal Ballet. In 1961 he became Director of the Stuttgart Ballet in Germany which he raised to international status.

Cunningham, Merce b. 1919 American modern dancer and choreographer who worked with the Martha Graham company before forming his own troupe. Cunningham is one of the most influential and gifted of modern dance choreographers.

Darrell, Peter b. 1929 English dancer and choreographer who was a founder member of Western Theatre Ballet in 1957. Since then he has guided the company which, in 1969, transferred to Glasgow and became the Scottish Ballet.

De Valois, Dame Ninette b. 1898 Irish-born dancer and choreographer. She was creator of Britain's Royal Ballet and its school.

Diaghilev, Serge 1872–1929 Russian man of the arts who did much to show Russian painting, music and above all ballet to the West. His Ballet Russe lasted from 1909 until his death, and its influence is still felt today.

Dowell, Anthony b. 1943 An English dancer of impeccable classical style. Principal dancer of The Royal Ballet.

Dudinskaya, Natalia b. 1912 Russian dancer who studied under Vaganova and became the principal dancer of the Leningrad State company. After her retirement she became one of the most celebrated teachers in the USSR.

Elssler, Fanny 1810–1884 Viennese-born dancer, one of the great stars of the Romantic ballet.

Festival Ballet An English company formed in 1950 by Alicia Markova and Anton Dolin. Since then it has toured widely presenting a popular repertory.

Flindt, Fleming b. 1936 Danish dancer and choreographer. He has been Director of the Royal Danish Ballet since 1965.

Fokine, Mikhail 1880–1942 Russian dancer and choreographer and one of the great innovators in ballet in this century. His creations for the Diaghilev company ensured the success of its first seasons.

Fonteyn, Dame Margot b. 1919 English dancer, Prima ballerina of The Royal Ballet throughout its formative years and probably the best-known and most popular of all contemporary dancers.

Graham, Martha b. 1893 American modern dancer and choreographer whose ballets and whose school have been of the utmost importance in developing the language and style of modern dance.

Grant, Alexander b. 1925 New Zealand dancer and one of The Royal Ballet's greatest character dancers. He created numerous roles in ballets, among them Alain in *La Fille mal Gardée* and Bottom in *The Dream*. Now Director of The National Ballet of Canada.

Grigorovitch, Yuri b. 1927 Russian dancer and choreographer, now Director of the Moscow Bolshoy Ballet for which he has created many stagings, notably *Spartacus*.

Harlem, Dance Theatre of, A company founded by Arthur Mitchell, soloist of the New York City Ballet, from students of the school of classical ballet which he started in 1968 in the Harlem district of New York.

Haydee, Marcia, Brazilian dancer who has been a principal of the Stuttgart Ballet since 1961 and became Director in 1976. Her great talent was an inspiration for many of John Cranko's finest ballets.

Helpmann, Sir Robert b. 1909 Australian dancer, choreographer and actor. He joined The Royal Ballet in 1933 and for the next twenty years was its principal male dancer and partner of Margot Fonteyn. He was a Director of the Australian Ballet from 1965 to 1976.

Imperial Society of Teachers of Dancing Founded in 1904, this English association embraces all forms of dancing. Incorporated in it are the Cecchetti Society and the Greek Dance Association; it has its own ballet syllabus and also encompasses ballroom and historical dancing.

Ivanov, Lev 1834–1901 Russian dancer and choreographer. He was second ballet master of the Imperial Ballet in St Petersburg and worked under Petipa's guidance. He is remembered today as choreographer of *The Nutcracker* and of the two lakeside scenes in *Swan Lake*.

Karsavina, Tamara b. 1885 Russian dancer, trained in St Petersburg where she early became a star of the Imperial ballet. In 1909 she was a member of the Ballet Russe company which conquered Paris. Resident in England since the 1920s she is the author of the marvellous book of ballet memoirs *Theatre Street*.

Kehlet, Niels b. 1938 Danish dancer of international reputation. He is an exceptional Bournonville stylist and also a superb dramatic dancer.

Kirstein, Lincoln b. 1907 American poet, writer on dance and the arts, and Director of the New York City Ballet, which he founded.

Kshessinskaya, Mathilde 1872–1971 Russian dancer who was the prima ballerina of the Imperial Russian Ballet for a quarter of a century, up to 1914. After the Russian Revolution she settled in Paris where she taught generations of dancers.

Lambert, Constant 1905–1951 English composer, conductor and author, Lambert was one of the architects of The Royal Ballet.

Lavrovsky, Leonid 1905–1967 Russian choreographer and artistic director of the Kirov Ballet and later the Bolshoy Ballet. His ballets – *Romeo and Juliet, The Stone Flower,* etc. – were very important in establishing the contemporary style of Soviet Ballet.

Liepa, Maris b. 1936 Latvian dancer, who has made a great career with the Bolshoy Ballet not only in classic roles but also as the villainous Crassus in *Spartacus.*

Lifar, Serge b. 1905 Russian-born dancer, choreographer and author, who joined the Ballet Russe in 1923 and became its principal dancer. He was Artistic Director of the Paris Opéra ballet from 1930 to 1958 during which time he revitalized that company.

MacMillan, Kenneth b. 1930 Scottish dancer and choreographer who made his first ballets for the Sadler's Wells Theatre Ballet in 1955. Since then he has been recognized as one of the major choreographers of our time, producing many important works for The Royal Ballet, of which he has been Director since 1970.

Madsen, Egon b. 1942 Danish dancer who has made his career since 1961 with the Stuttgart Ballet of which he is a principal. He combines romantic style and strong dramatic gifts.

Makarova, Natalia b. 1940 Russian dancer. She was star of the Leningrad Kirov Ballet before she defected to the West in London in 1970 and has since then danced all over the world, but chiefly in New York with the American Ballet Theatre and in London with The Royal Ballet.

Markova, Dame Alicia b. 1910 English dancer who joined the Diaghilev company at the age of fourteen. She was the first ballerina of The Royal Ballet and, later, after starring in America with the Ballet Russe and the Ballet Theater companies, she was a founder of the London Festival Ballet.

Massine, Leonide b. 1895 Russian dancer and choreographer who joined the Ballet Russe in 1913 and made his first ballet in 1915. In the 1930s he caused a storm of controversy with ballets danced to complete symphonies (Brahms, Tchaikovsky, Beethoven etc.) He is a great character choreographer.

Maximova, Ekaterina b. 1939 Russian dancer, one of the stars of the Bolshoy Ballet. She was coached in many roles by her great predecessor Ulanova.

Moreland, Barry b. 1943 Australian dancer and choreographer who made his first ballets for the London Contemporary Dance Theatre. Since 1971 he has been resident choreographer for the London Festival Ballet.

Morrice, Norman b. 1931 English dancer and choreographer, for many years Director of the Ballet Rambert. His ballets have shaped the image of the 'new' Rambert company which since 1966 has become increasingly contemporary in style.

Nerina, Nadia b. 1927 South African dancer who joined The Royal Ballet in 1946 and soon became a principal of the company. She excelled in the classics and Ashton created the role of Lise in *La Fille mal Gardée* for her. She retired in 1966.

Nijinsky, Vaslav 1888–1950 Russian dancer and choreographer. He was principal male dancer of the Diaghilev Ballet Russe from its first season in 1909 to 1917, with such enormous personal success that he has become a legendary figure. He created four very different and adventurous ballets, *L'Après-midi d'un faune*, *Le Sacre du Printemps Jeux* and *Tyl Eulenspiegel*.

Nureyev, Rudolf b. 1938 Russian dancer and producer. He was one of the most exciting young stars of the Kirov Ballet until he defected to the West in Paris in 1961. Since then he has been seen all over the world where his star personality has earned him enormous acclaim.

Pavlova, Anna 1881–1931 Russian dancer. Prima ballerina of the Imperial ballet and first ballerina of the Diaghilev Ballet Russe. From 1914 onwards she toured the world with her own company. One of the greatest dancers ballet has ever known.

Perrot, Jules 1810–1892 French dancer and choreographer who created superb dramatic ballets during the Romantic period, especially in London and St Petersburg.

Petipa, Marius 1818–1910 French dancer and choreographer who went to Russia in 1847 and thereafter became chief architect of the St Petersburg Ballet's greatness. His *Sleeping Beauty* (1890) is the masterpiece of ballet in the nineteenth century.

Seymour, Lynn b. 1939 Canadian dancer who joined The Royal Ballet School in 1954. Since then she has won international acclaim as a ballerina whose range is from pure classicism to the strong dramatic roles that have been created for her especially by Kenneth MacMillan. She is also a brilliant comedienne.

Sibley, Antoinette b. 1939 English dancer who entered The Royal Ballet School in 1956 and rose to become a principal of the company, dancing all the major classic roles as well as creating several important modern ones, such as Titania in *The Dream*.

Spessivtseva, Olga b. 1895 Russian dancer. An incomparable classical dancer, she was Diaghilev's first choice for his staging of *The Sleeping Princess* in London in 1921. Ill health terminated her career in 1939.

Sergueyev, Konstantin b. 1910 Russian dancer and choreographer who became principal male dancer of the Kirov Ballet and later Director of the company, for which he staged many important ballets.

Sergueeff, Nicholas 1876–1951 Russian dancer and ballet master, now remembered gratefully because after the Revolution he left St Petersburg bringing with him notebooks in which were written down the notation of much of the Imperial repertory. From these notebooks, Sergueeff was able to give the West the priceless heritage of nineteenth-century ballet.

Petit, Roland b. 1924 French dancer and choreographer. With his associates he was largely responsible for the new lease of life of the French ballet at the end of the Second World War. Since then he has worked in ballet, cinema and music hall where he has staged shows for his wife, Zizi Jeanmaire.

Rambert, Dame Marie b. 1888 Polish teacher and dancer. After working with the Diaghilev Ballet, Marie Rambert settled in London where she opened a school in 1920. From this developed the enterprising company which bears her name.

Robbins, Jerome b. 1918 American dancer and choreographer, whose ballets and musicals have been internationally acclaimed.

Royal Academy of Dancing Founded in London in 1920, the Academy is now devoted to maintaining teaching standards of ballet throughout the world.

St Léon, Arthur 1821–1870 French dancer and choreographer. He created ballets throughout Europe and was chief ballet master in St Petersburg from 1860–69.

Taglioni, Marie 1804–1884 Italian dancer who came to epitomize the Romantic style.

Taylor, Paul b. 1930 American dancer and choreographer and principal dancer of the Graham company. In 1954 he founded his own troupe for which he has created a series of dance works which are recognized as being among the finest of our time.

Tetley, Glen b. 1926 American dancer and choreographer who has worked chiefly in Europe. His ballets for the Nederlands Dans Theater and the Ballet Rambert, among others, have been very influential. He was Director of the Stuttgart Ballet of 1974–76.

Tharp, Twyla b. 1942 American dancer and choreographer whose imaginative power and amazing vocabulary of movement mark her as one of the most exciting creators of today.

Ulanov, Galina b. 1910 Russian dancer who was the legendary ballerina first of the Kirov and later of the Bolshoy Ballet in Moscow.

Vaganova, A Y 1897–1951 A ballerina of the St Petersburg Ballet and a crucial figure in the creation of Soviet Ballet after the Revolution. Her teaching method is universally followed in Russia and it is the basis for much of the physical splendour of Soviet dancing today.

Vasiliev, Vladimir b. 1940 Russian dancer who typifies the heroic and brilliant style of the Bolshoy Ballet.

Vestris, Auguste 1760–1842 Son and pupil of Gaëtan Vestris, he became in his turn one of the most acclaimed dancers of his age and in due time a teacher at the Paris Opéra where he taught Elssler and appeared in one performance with Taglioni.

Vestris, Gaëtan 1729–1808 Italian dancer who became the greatest star of the Paris Opéra of his day.

Villella, Edward b. 1936 American dancer and one of the first virtuoso male stars of the New York City Ballet.

Van Praagh, Dame Peggy b. 1910 English dancer and teacher who played a significant role in the early development of British ballet and became Assistant Director of the Sadler's Wells Theatre Ballet. From 1962–75 she was Director of the Australian Ballet.

Vyroubova, Nina b. 1921 Russian dancer whose career lay in France, where she became, in turn, star of the Paris Opéra and of the Grand Ballet du Marquis de Cuevas.

Wall, David b. 1946 English dancer who was a pupil of The Royal Ballet School and became one of the youngest-ever principals of The Royal Ballet.

INDEX

Figures in italics refer to pictures